Nuclear Futurism

The work of art in the age of
remainderless destruction

Nuclear
Futurism

The work of art in the age of
remainderless destruction

Liam Sprod

Winchester, UK
Washington, USA

First published by Zero Books, 2012
Zero Books is an imprint of John Hunt Publishing Ltd., Laurel House, Station Approach,
Alresford, Hants, SO24 9JH, UK
office1@jhpbooks.net
www.johnhuntpublishing.com
www.zero-books.net

For distributor details and how to order please visit the 'Ordering' section on our website.

Text copyright: Liam Sprod 2011
Front cover photograph copyright: Linda Persson 2012

ISBN: 978 1 78099 433 8

A CIP catalogue record for this book is available from the British Library.

Design: Stuart Davies

Printed and bound by CPI Group (UK) Ltd, Croydon, CR0 4YY

We operate a distinctive and ethical publishing philosophy in all
areas of our business, from our global network of authors to
production and worldwide distribution.

CONTENTS

"The series of weapon tests had fused the sand in layers, and the pseudological strata condensed the brief epochs, microseconds in duration, of the thermonuclear age. "The key to the past lies in the present." Typically the island inverted this geologist's maxim. Here the key to the present lay in the future. The island was a fossil of time future, its bunkers and blockhouses illustrating the principle that the fossil record of life is one of amour and the exoskeleton."

J.G. Ballard 'The Terminal Beach.'

Acknowledgements

There are a few people who must be thanked for the roles they played in the writing and publication of this book. First and foremost are my parents, whose constant love and support is the foundation upon which all of my thinking is built. Likewise, Linda Persson, who has taught me more about art than I ever learnt from reading the books that went into writing this one. If it were not for her this would remain an unread ruin and all my future thinking unthought. Jeff Malpas and Dirk Meure from the University of Tasmania both played a large part in the writing of the initial notes and ideas that later became this book. Finally, many thanks to Zero Books for publishing the book at a time when the ideas it contains seem more important than ever for the future-no-longer-to-come.

Introduction

Terminal Documents

"Kaldren chattered away, explaining the significance of the so-called Terminal Documents. 'They're end prints, Powers, final statements, the products of total fragmentation. When I've got enough together I'll build a new world for myself out of them.'"

J.G. Ballard 'The Voices of Time.'

Somewhere in the twentieth century the future failed and the possibility of the new retreated into the insipid instant gratification of the now. This failure has left culture and philosophy in a terminal condition, dominated by a series of discourses of ends: from the end of poetry in the horror of Auschwitz, through the end of television in Timișoara, Romania, the end of art, postmodernism's end of meta-narratives, to the declaration of the end of history with the collapse of the Berlin Wall and the supposed triumph of liberal democracy, or more precisely, capitalism.[1] The last of these, the victory of capitalism and the end of history, represents the ultimate failure of the future, for it goes beyond the discursive domain of a particular aspect of culture and takes aim at the very progression of development itself. Likewise, it perhaps contains the conditions for the proliferation of particular ends. This reinforces the assertion by Fredric Jameson that it is now "easier to imagine the end of the world than to imagine the end of capitalism" and his reversal, that the result of this leaves only "the attempt to imagine capitalism by way of imagining the end of the world."[2] Under the stasis of late capitalism, which was achieved long before the final decline of the Soviet Union, where it is impossible to imagine a future history, the apocalyptic discourses of ends multiply as they are infected one after the other with the terminal logic of capitalism.[3] This also accounts for the proliferation of apocalyptic imagery from ecological collapse to financial meltdowns and terrorist or state driven Armageddon. However, within this pessimistic production of apocalyptic discourses, there is perhaps the chance to reinvigorate and return to the future and to build a new world out of the fragments of its very failure.

The particular fragments selected for this project are the central end of history and the end of art, these are contrasted with the apocalyptic discourses of remainderless nuclear war and the artistic avant-garde of the Italian futurists, who also aimed to escape history by the very forces of the new that they found in the modern technology which was to shape the century of ends. It is this constellation that gives this book its name and provides the theory of nuclear futurism. Just as it was the impulse of the early twentieth century avant-garde that lead to the declaration of the end of art in the later stages of that same century, so too was it the ideological conflict between communism and capitalism that formed the nuclear tensions and raised the specter of a nuclear apocalypse, as well as the possibility of the declaration of the end of history. Running throughout this fragmentary constellation are the ideas of technology and literature as writing, the latter being the technology of language itself and the possibility of both this book and philosophy.

The new future built from these fragments is undoubtedly a philosophical one, that is, one built through philosophy. As an element of temporality in general, the future cannot help but be subject to the metaphysical examinations of philosophy. In particular, it is the works of German philosopher Martin Heidegger and French philosopher Jacques Derrida that form the base of this new vision of the future. Both of these philosophers are concerned with history, the history of philosophy and the possibilities and impossibilities of temporality and the future opened up by these histories. Derrida specifically engages with the issue of nuclear war and remainderless destruction in a little-read paper from 1984 entitled 'No Apocalypse, Not Now (Full Speed Ahead, Seven Missiles, Seven Missives).'[4] This paper aimed to establish a new discourse of nuclear criticism at a time when the apocalyptic tensions of the Cold War were at their highest, and the end of history was waiting just around the corner. For all of its avant-garde intentions this discourse effectively starts and ends with this short paper. However, it can still act as a conduit through which the entirety of Derrida's philosophical project of deconstruction can be examined, and out of which it is possible to construct a new version of the future as a progressive event, happening now, which is no longer trapped in a beyond, forever sealed off by the fragmentation of time through the discourses of ends.

The reconfiguration of the future as a futural and progressive event instead of an anticipated to come, which always remains in the future and never becomes an actuality, is the central argument of this book. The best articulation of this sort of event is found in Heidegger's interrelated philosophies of art, technology and language, and this returns to the juxtaposition of futurism and the end of art. Heidegger's concept of the event is part of his wider critique of the history of philosophy, which was the basis for Derrida's deconstructive method. By keeping this in mind, it becomes apparent how the development of the possibility of a new future also contains within itself a confrontation with the problem of the history of philosophy as a critical project, opposed to the creativity of art and the path it opens for the future.

This is the path this book aims to follow. Not only as a critique of the static and derelict pessimism of the end times, which allow apocalyptic dangers and horror to persist in the present without the possibility of escape; but as a positive futurity that opens up the present to the future and an escape from the discourses of ends. Never has the possibility of this path been more necessary than in the wasteland of the apocalyptic present. It is this fundamentally philosophical vision of futurity that must rest at the base of any critique of the stasis of the present condition of the world, be that economic, ideological, artistic or poetic. Only through the writing of the future can these critiques function, and only through the sending of that opening up can a new, futural world be built.

The structure of the book follows a path from these problems of the future towards their ends, but perhaps does not need to be read quite so directly. The first Chapter explains the problems of the future in its temporal dimension and the dual issues of the end of history and the end of art. The next two Chapters develop the similarities between futurism and nuclear criticism and the way that each of these discourses confronts the future. Chapters four, five and six examine the wider philosophical work of Jacques Derrida, specifically through deconstruction, the ghost and experimental literature respectively. Aptly enough for a philosopher of writing, reading Derrida is always somewhat like learning to read anew. As each word and every work takes on a new meaning in light of its place and part within the wider scope of the sentence or structure. Thus the reader may find that these three Chapters provide the wider philosophical context for some of the specific ideas that Derrida developed with regard to nuclear criticism and thus they can be read both as an introduction to Derrida's work in general, but also as a specific comment on the problems raised by nuclear criticism and the temporality of the future. Chapters seven and nine examine the work of Martin Heidegger, through his theories of art and language respectively, and develop his idea of the event as an alternative temporality that escapes the problems of futurity. These are joined by an excursion into the theory of the museum in Chapter eight, which returns to the issues of the archive and its relation to nuclear criticism and the futurists. Chapters ten and eleven bring art and history face to face with the apocalyptic nature of their own ends and elaborates the reconfigured image of the future by which nuclear futurism aims to escape this apocalyptic stasis.

Chapter I

The (Non) Event of 1984

1984 is an ominous year. It is the symbol of the future. This, of course, is in reference to George Orwell's book *1984*; the future dystopia which has still not occurred. Although the calendar tells us that we have long since passed the date, in many ways *1984* still remains in the future. All futures, it seems, must fall prey to this flaw, be they utopian or dyspotian. The future can never be now. It is always future futurity, forever to-come and never present. A certain way of thinking about the future is revealed here, the future anterior, where a future event is talked about as if it has happened already and can now be observed from a time after its happening: 'the future will have been like'. However, this is only one mode of thinking about the future, a mode that may have ended in 1984. In fact, it is possible to say that the beginning of the future will have been in 1984. This event of the future has in many ways been forgotten, or worse still is destined merely to be remembered, to become part of history.

In 1984 a small colloquium took place at Cornell University on a newly created type of criticism called Nuclear Criticism. This period of time was possibly the hottest the Cold War ever became aside from the Cuban Missile Crisis of 1962. Just a year before President Regan had denounced the USSR as the "Evil Empire" and instigated the Strategic Defense Initiative (SDI) or 'Star Wars', a plan to create a defense shield over America to protect it from potential nuclear attack.[1] Subsequently, this plan was reinvigorated by George W. Bush and is still being implemented across Europe, much to the disgust of Russia. Only three years later in 1987 the nuclear stockpile of the USSR reached its maximum at 40 723 weapons, while the USA had 23 490.[2] Amidst this climate the Cornell colloquium sought to examine how these conscious and unconscious nuclear fears played into various texts, and what might be the critical response to these texts.[3] At the spearhead of this new discourse was Jacques Derrida who presented a paper entitled 'No Apocalypse, Not Now (Full Speed Ahead, Seven Missiles, Seven Missives)', which in many ways may be regarded as the founding manifesto of nuclear criticism. As the term 'founding manifesto' implies, the colloquium and the subsequent discourse of nuclear criticism saw itself as an important new mode of discourse which would change the nature of criticism itself, bringing forth a new age of critique.

However, only a handful of years later the Cold War was to come to a sudden end with the collapse of the USSR; an event which Francis Fukuyama was to describe as the end of history. Certainly, to the extent that it depends on the threat of imminent nuclear destruction, it seems that the end of the Cold War was indeed the end of nuclear criticism. More importantly, what also seemed to end was the very utopian impulse at the core of nuclear criticism. For Fukuyama, what the end of history represented was the end of change, the end of new modes of thought, of ideology. The production of ideology, and the violence associated with these differing ideologies found its apotheosis in that which was the very subject of nuclear criticism. Fukuyama writes:

> The twentieth century saw the developed world descend into a paroxysm of ideological violence, as liberalism contended first with the remnants of absolutism, then bolshevism and fascism, and finally an updated Marxism that threatened to lead to the ultimate apocalypse of nuclear war.[4]

Of course there is much more to the idea of the end of history than the avoidance of nuclear war. But what this shows is that with the collapse of the Soviet Union came an apparent end of the nuclear issue. The conditions that seemed to define the domain of nuclear criticism also collapsed. The future of nuclear criticism, in both senses of the word, was abandoned to the history of ideas. Many would say that the disappearance of the small movement of nuclear criticism is a fair enough price to pay for the end of the threat of imminent nuclear war. However, for Fukuyama, there is much more at stake in the end of history. He concludes: "In the post-historical period there will be neither art nor philosophy, just the perpetual caretaking of the museum of human history."[5] The end of nuclear criticism is merely indicative of the wider ends of philosophy and art, which are much more troubling thoughts.

Along with the end of history, the end of art has been mentioned many times before Fukuyama took up the idea. Notably, Arthur C. Danto suggested it in the pivotal year of 1984. Danto himself was well aware of the Orwellian importance of this year, and in fact was to play on this very fact in his in depth examination of the end of art.[6] For Danto the year 1984 was defined by the symbolic non-event of Orwell's dystopia. This represented the end of Orwell's fictional historical progression. 1984 was no longer the future, and the future, now a reality, was part of history.

Danto's thesis on art is similar to Fukuyama's, that there can no longer be any historical progression within art. This does not mean that art will stop being produced, but that the history of art has come to its conclusion, that art as an historical progression had arrived at its final point. All art produced after the end of art will not not be art but will be *post-historical* art. What this means for Danto is that "[n]o art is any longer historically mandated as against any other art. Nothing is any more true as art than anything else, nothing especially more historically false than anything else."[7] The reason for this, Danto argues, is that art has become completely self-conscious and has completely exhausted its own historical possibility, that is, it has realized its own conditions of possibility. Any art is now possible and it is permissible

8

that anything is art.[8] It is no longer the domain of artistic production to discriminate between something as art and something that is not. Although Danto did not identify this end of art until 1984, the event itself had taken place some twenty years before against the backdrop of the sixties. Danto writes:

> The sixties was a paroxysm of styles, in the course of whose contention, it seems to me - and this was the basis of my speaking of the "end of art" in the first place - it gradually became clear, first through the *nouveaux realistes* and pop, that there was no special way works of art had to look in contrast to what I had designated "mere real things."[9]

The ultimate example that Danto gives is Andy Warhol's *Brillo Box*, an exact copy of the Brillo boxes that could be purchased at any supermarket. It is interesting to note that Danto uses the same language to express events in the art world as Fukuyama uses to express those in the ideological world - the various paroxysms which appeared before the supposed end of these narratives.

In particular what these two events, Warhol's *Brillo Box* and the violent paroxysm of styles, indicate are the death spasm of what Danto calls the age of manifestos. The age of manifestos was characterized by an attempt to define what exactly art was and to give an articulation of how one form of art, be it dada, surrealism, or the *maschinkunst* of Tatalin, was the ultimate form of art. The various manifestos and their statements on art were the way in which artists grappled with the philosophy of art, the way in which they sought to define their art as the truth about art. What Danto sees as the end of art is the end of the possibility of any such claims, the ultimate truth about art is that anything is permissible, the philosophical justification is no longer an artistic endeavor, but is explicitly philosophical. This is the Hegelian notion that in the movement of *Geist* art will be sumlimated by philosophy (the full Hegelian influence and implications of these 'end of' narratives will be returned to in Chapter 11). In a certain way, as Fukuyama's triumph of ideological freedom represented the end of history, the stylistic freedom that the violent paroxysm of the sixties gave way to is the ultimate representation of the end of art. After the end of art the manifesto will become redundant, because it is philosophically invalid to claim the philosophical superiority of one form of art over another. It will no longer be possible to judge artwork by the historical situation or movement within which it is located. In many ways Danto's theory on the end of art ties up with what is often called the crisis in the avant-garde. Theorists such as Peter Bürger and Andreas Huyssen have suggested that the avant-garde is now merely of historical significance.[10] This idea is more empirical than that of Danto, it is merely necessary to point to the appropriation of various avant-garde moments by the culture industry. The progressive and radical nature of the avant-garde and its search for the new has been sold out. The art industry, by the very freedom Danto rejoices in, has made experimentation impossible. To co-opt Fukuyama's phrase, and give it a somewhat literal meaning, all that is possible is the caretaking of the museum that is the culture industry.

Another theorist, Krzysztof Ziarek, rejects the idea of this crisis along with any idea of the end of art. In his book *The Historicity of Experience: Modernity, the avant-garde and the event*[11] he connects the Heideggerian notion of the artwork as an event, and his analysis of technology, with Benjamin's critique of the art work in the age of mechanical reproduction. As a result of this conjunction he develops a theory in which the avant-garde artwork reveals the historicity of its own event as a critique of modern technology. Rather than Danto's view that the manifesto driven avant-garde was driven by its own historical context, Ziarek claims that the experience of the avant-garde artwork is engaged in an active historicization and critique of its own historical context. In particular, he sees this in terms of the critique of modernity and the technological experience of the world. For him, avant-garde artwork is still possible, there has been no end of art although there may well have been a decrease in truly avant-garde art, as a result of the process of the technological domination of the world, which does not allow the world to be revealed in its historical context, but merely as the Heideggerian notion of standing reserve. For Ziarek, although not necessarily therefore for Heidegger, this dominance of the technological mode of thought would indeed be the end of history in terms of the possibility of any historicist critique as by its very essence, technology does not reveal its own historical conditions of possibility. Hence, it is up to the avant-garde in some form to rail against the technological. This ideological conflict between the technological mode of thought and the avant-garde is played out by the fascination that avant-garde artists have always had for various forms of technology. The full importance of these similar yet conflicting theories of art and the explicit connection to Heidegger's thought on technology will be explicitly addressed in Chapter 7.

To view these synchronous events of 1984, the year, reveals what was identified above as the problematic of *1984* as a symbol of the future. On one hand the Cornell colloquium celebrated the creation of a new discourse. On the other, Danto announced the end of the possibility of new discourses; an end which only a few years later would engulf the domain that defined nuclear criticism. This is the event, in time, and also the non-event of the future of 1984. The end of history is also the end of the future, the end of the possibility of the new. Is it still possible to have such a conception of the future after the (non) event of 1984, and if so how would such a future manifest itself and contrast itself with the idea of the end of history in particular as the end of historical, or historicist art?

Chapter 2

The New Beauty of Speed

The small early twentieth century artistic movement known as futurism provides a problematic point for the theory of art and the avant-garde as put forward above by both Danto and Ziarek. Futurism emerged in 1909 with the publication of its founding manifesto, which was also possibly the very founding of the artistic manifesto, on the front page of the Parisian daily *Le Figaro*.[1] Written by Filippo Tommaso Marinetti, the self-proclaimed "caffeine of Europe,"[2] this manifesto was an organized attack on the history of art. It declared a new form of art, an art of the future which would embrace dynamism, speed, violence and, above all, the machine and technology.[3] Futurism is problematic for the above theorists due to its declaration of total war against history. It neither seeks to give itself some sort of historical mandate against other forms of art in the way which Danto claims is characteristic of the age of manifestos, nor does it seek to create some sort of historicist critique in the way which Ziarek describes. In fact, futurism's championing of technology contrasts in almost every way with Ziarek's characterization of the avant-garde. The key to this problematic lies in the fact that futurism rejects history and historicism of all sorts in favor of the future. Futurism did not create itself as a style (although undoubtedly a futurist style did exist albeit in a highly problematic form). Rather, it set itself in opposition to other styles. It did not take part in the growing paroxysm of styles in the age of manifestos, but in fact drew its energy from this paroxysm itself. It was from this violent and dynamic confrontation that the destruction of history and the arrival of the future would grow. In exactly this way nuclear criticism did not set itself up as a new ideology against the two sides of the Cold

War, but instead located itself at the very nexus of their confrontation, in the middle of the ideological paroxysm itself. Nuclear criticism emerged and proclaimed itself the criticism of the future at precisely the moment when the nuclear tension was the greatest, in an identical way in which futurism declared itself the art of the future amidst the growing tension amongst the proliferation of styles such as cubism, expressionism, fauvism, and impressionism. Interestingly there are many further points of comparison between these two discourses of futurism and nuclear criticism. In many ways both are set against the problematic of the (non) event of 1984, both are the paradoxical champions of the future, which have been doomed to history and forgotteness. However, by examining this comparison it is perhaps possible to reinvigorate both the ideas of the future and of the avant-garde.

The above similarities between nuclear criticism and futurism are what might be called formal similarities, that is, similarities between the conditions within which they functioned. However, the real points of interest arise when what might be called the similarities of content are examined. These will reveal how these two discourses actually function. There are three main points of similarity. The first of these is the idea of technology as the catalyst of the future. The futurists saw the future in all forms of modern technology and machinery; however they themselves were not engineers or mechanics competent in the maintenance and development of this Promethean technology. Likewise the domain of nuclear criticism is fundamentally defined by a technological innovation, the nuclear weapon and its use in modern warfare. With this technological innovation, however, there is a much more imminent risk. However, like the futurists, the people who are engaged in nuclear criticism are not themselves involved in what Derrida identifies as the techno-scientifico-militaro-diplomatic configuration of nuclear warfare. They are philosophers, theorists, poets and authors of all sorts.

This technology of total nuclear destruction reveals the second point of similarity, which is the idea of the destruction of history. This idea is very literal for the nuclear critics; a total nuclear war would be one of remainderless destruction. Quite simply, it would wipe out every trace of human history. For the futurists this idea was much more metaphorical. They wanted to escape the burden of artistic convention in order to produce an art that could reflect the way in which technology allowed an escape from the bondage of the past. In his founding manifesto Marinetti writes:

> It is from Italy that we launch through the world this violently upsetting, incendiary manifesto of ours. With it today we establish *Futurism* because we want to free this land from its smelly gangrene of professors, archaeologists, ciceroni, and antiquarians.[4]

This idea was of particular importance in the historical context of an Italy, which bore the heavy legacy of both the Renaissance and the glory of the Roman Empire, and was attempting to forge a new identity in the modern era. Despite this destruction, neither futurism nor nuclear criticism are purely negative doctrines.

This leads to the third point of similarity, that is, the importance of speed as the force of the new. This is a point so important to Marinetti that he makes it twice in his founding manifesto. Firstly, at point four, he writes:

> We say that the world's magnificence has been enriched by a new beauty; the beauty of speed. A racing car whose hood is adorned with great pipes, like serpents of explosive breath - a roaring car that seems to ride on grapeshot - is more beautiful than the *Victory of Samothrace*.[5]

The aesthetics of futurism are clearly defined by the conjunction of speed as an aspect of technology. However, this is not the only way in which speed is important. It also has a much more radical metaphysical implication. At point eight of the manifesto Marinetti writes:

> We stand on the last promontory of the centuries! ... Why should we look back, when what we want is to break down the mysterious doors of the Impossible? Time and space died yesterday. We already live in the absolute, because we have created eternal, omnipresent speed.[6]

There are three important elements of this statement. The first is the proclamation of the death of time and space, two of the great pillars of philosophy, and in particular of the way in which the world is experienced. The second is the manifestation of the absolute, which itself is an important philosophical idea (this point will arise in Chapter 10, which is concerned with the connection between art, the absolute and the sublime). Finally, it outlines the way in which these two elements are a result of speed as the new defining feature of the world: not just as the technological speed of the racing car, but as an ontological condition. This distinction fits within the Heideggerian schema of the ontico-ontological difference, that is, the difference between particular scientific, technological, cultural or historical knowledge of the world (which is ontic) and the conditions of possibility of both the world and that knowledge (which is ontological).[7] The experience of the speed of the racing car is a purely ontic understanding of speed, which is intimately connected to a deeper ontological understanding of speed. It is by examining the connections between this ontico-ontological difference that a new logic of speed may be arise.

This is exactly what Derrida is getting at with the nuclear aphorism of his first missive, "[a]t the beginning there will have been speed."[8] Like Marinetti's formulation of speed in the

'Founding Manifesto of Futurism' the way in which Derrida formulates speed is two fold. Firstly, he points out how the logic of nuclear war as an arms race is defined by speed. He writes:

> Whether it is the arms race or orders given to start a war that is itself dominated by that economy of speed throughout all zones of its technology, a gap of a few seconds may decide, irreversibly, the fate of what is still now and then called humanity - plus the fate of a few other species.[9]

Like the racing car of futurism, the technology that nuclear criticism is engaged with is defined by speed on every level. This includes the speed at which new weapons are developed, the speed at which strategic decisions are made and the speed of the weapons themselves as they fly towards their targets. Nuclear war, more than any other sort of war, is defined throughout by the experience of speed. However, as with futurism this logic of speed cuts deeper still. With the omnipresence of speed within the nuclear discourse also comes the rethinking of time and space as prefigured by Marinetti. To quote Derrida at length:

> Are we having today, *another*, a different experience of speed? Is our relation to time and to motion qualitatively different? Or must we speak of prudently of an extraordinary - although qualitatively homogenous - acceleration of the same experience? And what temporality do we have in mind when we put the question that way? Can we take the question seriously without re-elaborating all the problematics of time and motion, from Aristotle to Heidegger by way of Augustine, Kant, Husserl, Einstein, Bergson, and so on? So my first formulation of the question of speed was simplistic. It opposed quantity and quality as *if* a quantitative transformation - the crossing of certain thresholds of acceleration within the general machinery of a culture, with all the

techniques for handling, recording, and storing information - could not induce qualitative mutations, as *if every* invention were not the invention of a process of acceleration or, at the very least, a new experience of speed.[10]

Here Derrida explicitly spells out what is at stake in this new double experience, both as a reformulation of the idea of speed and as a new experience which will be speed itself. What is required is a rethinking of the very foundations of temporality itself, or, to give a literal meaning to Marinetti's catchphrase, time and space died yesterday.

In his first missile/missive where Derrida declares, in his own way, the possible death of time and space and the new experience of speed, he also returns to the problem of the future that is central to the (non) event of 1984. This is most obvious in the strange phrasing of the nuclear aphorism 'at the beginning there will have been speed.' As Ken Ruthven points out this rather curious idiom reveals the way in which nuclear criticism does not think in terms of the future anterior but in the future perfect.[11] 'At the beginning there will have been speed', itself a rewriting of the moment of Genesis' 'in the beginning was the word', does not allow any space between the beginning and the end, within which the present tense could operate. Nor does it speculate something beyond the end; that would both open up the future tense - 'there will be speed and then x' - and allow the beginning to be referred to in the past tense.

This very phrasing is a critique of the way in which the temporality of the future has been considered since the time of Plato. It is exactly this point that Richard Klein picks up on when he speculates on the future of nuclear criticism in the immediate period after the end of the Cold War. Under these conditions, when Klein writes about the future of nuclear criticism the phrase has a double meaning. On one hand he is speculating on what sort of a future there is for the discourse of nuclear criticism in the world after the end of the Cold War. On the other hand he is examining how it is that nuclear criticism envisions, or possibly re-envisions, the idea of the future within its discourse. The future perfect of nuclear criticism replaces the future anterior that has dominated thought of the future.

The idea of the future anterior has its roots in Plato's *Philebus* where thought about the future is understood as a form of mimetic representation. As a re-presentation the future must already be understood as having a past; as anticipation that which is anticipated must be understood as already having happened in order for it to be represented in the present.[12] As an aside, it is interesting to note that this mimetic understanding of anticipation as future memory also implicitly contains a correspondence theory of truth and a mimetic understanding of art. This configuration between the future, truth and art will become a central issue of this book, which will be returned to several times. Understanding nuclear criticism via the paradigm of the future anterior has developed into the theory of the nuclear sublime. The sublime is an aesthetic theory about the way in which the unthinkable may be represented in art; this emphasis on representation shows how the idea of the nuclear sublime is still within both the mimetic framework of representation and the correspondence theory of truth.

Klein's proposal is much more radical. The possibility of remainderless destruction that nuclear criticism presents does not allow for it to be understood in terms of the future anterior. Quite literally there is no anterior to the possibility of total nuclear war because nothing will be left, there will be no after, and definitely no possibility of any such viewpoint. For Klein, what this possibility provokes is a need to rethink the way in which the future is considered, a way in which a logic of the future may function in the face of total nuclear destruction, and this is precisely the task of the future of nuclear criticism.[13] In precisely the same way, the (non) event of 1984 is a representation of the disintegration of the future anterior that is the utopian mode of thought. However, the year 1984 and the advent of nuclear criticism also saw the rethinking of the future in term of the future perfect of speed. In order to understand how the future may be rethought in terms of speed, and also to draw out the conjunction of nuclear criticism and futurism, it is necessary to understand the process that led Derrida to his proclamation.

Chapter 3

The Fabulously Textual Nuclear War

Derrida's discussion of the nuclear issue is structured around what he calls the aporia of the nuclear referent.[1] The term referent implies that this argument is structured around a textual understanding of the nuclear issue. As has been pointed out above, an apparent problem for the nuclear critic is the fact that he or she is not directly connected with the techno-scientifico-militaro-diplomatic configuration of nuclear warfare. Instead, the nuclear critic is an expert in discourse and texts. However, as Derrida points out, this conflict of competence is not as problematic as it first appears. This is because the nuclear issue is "a phenomenon whose essential feature is that of being *fabulously textual*, through and through."[2] As with the above formulation of speed, this textual nature of nuclear criticism works within the two levels of the ontico-ontological difference. At the ontic level nuclear warfare is utterly dependent upon structures of information, communication and language.[3] As the different elements of the nuclear configuration, at the levels of diplomacy, intelligence and research, all function through these structures. This is the level at which most nuclear criticism functions; the critique of the various rhetorical structures which surround the nuclear issue, be they, fictional, diplomatic, scientific, etc. Analysis at merely this level is problematic because by its rhetorical nature it falls into the mode of gossip and *doxa* (opinion). This is where the techno-scientifico-militaro-diplomatic incompetence of the nuclear critic is revealed as they descend into sophistry and psycho-rhetoric.[4] In order to avoid this, the way in which the essential textual nature of the nuclear issue goes beyond merely the ontic and reaches to the level of the ontological must be taken into account.

Nuclear war as the total engagement of nuclear warfare, rather than the extension of regular war by a single nuclear action such as the bombing of Japan at the end of the Second World War, is fabulously textual precisely because it has not taken place; it is only possible to talk and write about it. The result of this is that "the terrifying reality of the nuclear conflict can only be the signified referent, never the real referent (present or past) of a discourse or a text."[5] It is textual because that is all it can be - a text that is its own self-referent. It is fabulous because as a pure text it is a story, a myth, a fiction, a fantasy. This is the ontological nature of nuclear war as fabulously textual. There is a clear schism at work here. This 'ontological' nature of nuclear war seems to go against the very meaning of ontological itself: What of the 'reality' of the nuclear missiles sitting in their silos, the 'reality' of the sheer destructive power of these missiles. This cannot be denied, but the distinction between the nuclear age and the fiction of nuclear war must be maintained. The missiles may be real but this reality is determined by the fiction of a text. It is the fiction of nuclear war which motivates both the techno-scientific inventiveness and also the politico-diplomatic structures and strategies. This ontological formulation of nuclear war as fabulously textual allows the nuclear critic to not only critique the nuclear discourse but also the ontological itself. As Derrida writes:

"Reality," let's say the encompassing institution of the nuclear age, is constructed on a fable, on the basis of an event that has never happened (except in fantasy, and that is not nothing at all), an event of which one can only speak, an event whose advent remains an invention by men (in all the senses of the word "invention") or which, rather, remains to be invented.[6]

The play on the senses of invention here refers to firstly the technological nature of invention and secondly the fantastic, or phantasmal, nature of the text as a work of fiction. By situating this play on invention within the above critique of ontology - the way in which the 'real' inventions of nuclear techno-science are determined by the fabulous invention of a text - Derrida is also foreshadowing a critique of the essence of technology as *techne*.

The integration of the ontico-ontological difference within the textuality of nuclear war means that while at one level the text will *be* and at the same time *produce* 'reality,' at another it will also allow a way of understanding and interpreting reality, a way clearly within the domain of the nuclear critic as a mechanic of texts.

The competency of nuclear criticism, and indeed the textualization of nuclear war itself, reveals the importance of nuclear criticism and the way in which is must relate to philosophy in general. This is not only because it deals with the possibility or anticipation of the remainderless destruction of humanity, but because "the anticipation of nuclear war (dreaded as the fantasy, or phantasm, of a remainderless destruction) installs humanity - and through all sorts of relays even defines the essence of modern humanity - in its rhetorical condition."[7] This is a sort of symmetry between the textual nature of nuclear war and the essence of modern humanity as rhetorical, which defines the competency of the nuclear critic as a scholar of the humanities. This symmetry also, and this will become more apparent below, means that nuclear criticism as textual analysis is also a way of critiquing the structures of technology and diplomacy which it contains. This is precisely the point which Derrida is making in the second of his missives/missiles when he writes: "We [nuclear critics] can therefore consider ourselves competent because the sophistication of the nuclear strategy can never do without the sophistry of belief and the rhetorical simulation of a text."[8] It is thus through Derrida's rhetorical exploration of the nuclear issue as a textual one that the critique of time and space will develop.

In this way, by examining the rhetorical simulation of the text of nuclear war, Derrida is able to develop what he calls the "aporia of the nuclear referent."[9] Examining the conditions of literature motivates Derrida's first formulation of this aporia. There are two important elements or conditions to literature, without which it would not be possible. The first is the stockpiling and building up of "an objective archive over and above any traditional oral base."[10] This is the continual collection and storage of texts in the various institutions of archives, which means that the text is objectified in a way in which oral texts cannot be. The second condition is the "development of a positive law implying authors' rights, the identification of the signatory, of the corpus, names, titles, the distinction between the original and the copy, the original and the plagiarized version, and so forth."[11] In short, this is the judicial archive of the legality of the author, which inextricably entwines the author and the text. These two conditions are vital to the continual existence of literature. However, these two conditions point toward an interesting relationship between literature and nuclear war. As Derrida points out:

> Now what allows us perhaps to think the uniqueness of nuclear war, its being-for-the-first-time-and-perhaps-for-the-last-time, its absolute inventiveness, what it prompts us to think even if it remains a decoy, a belief, a phantasmatic projection, is obviously the possibility of an irreversible destruction, leaving no traces, of the juridico-literary archive - that is, total destruction of the basis of literature and criticism.[12]

While humanity, and thus in some sense poetry and the sciences, may survive the total destruction of the archive, literature may not. This is because poetry and the sciences are not dependent upon the archive but have a referent beyond their own conditions of possibility. Whereas literature, insofar as it is dependent upon the archive, can only produce itself as a fiction dependent upon the possibility of this archive; and indeed is itself constituted by the story this archivizing act tells.

The "phantasmatic projection" of this quote also foreshadows the figure of the specter or ghost, which will appear some 10 years after the presentation of 'No Apocalypse, Not Now' in Derrida's book *Specters of Marx*.[13] The specter, as the return of a ghost who also appears for the first time and the last time, sets out more explicitly what is at stake in the disjunction of temporality and the disruption of ontology that functions not just in Derrida's engagement with the questions of nuclear war, but also within his philosophical project as a whole. Befitting its temporal logic, this figure will return in Chapter 5.

Derrida sees a strong affinity between this hypothetical total and remainderless destruction of the archive and his own philosophical method of deconstruction. In much the same way as the destruction of history was the very condition of possibility of the futurist doctrine of the future of art, deconstruction seeks to reveal the fantastic nature and radical historicity of the texts it is deconstructing: texts that in their totality are none other than literature. What the hypothesis of the total and remainderless destruction of the archive reveals is the immense threat to literature by nuclear catastrophe. This radical precariousness in turn reveals the radical historicity of the conditions of literature. However, at the same time, the possibility of the absolute destruction of literature allows the totality and completeness of literature to appear, that is, to think it as the wholeness of its self as nothing other than self-reference (although it must be remembered that the nothing is just as important in this statement). What the combination of these two elements produces is an understanding of the historicity of literature as a sort of historical fiction, or, as literature itself. The possibility of understanding literature in its totality is dependent upon the hypothesis of its total destruction. This is what prompts Derrida to declare that the "historicity of literature is contemporaneous through and through, or rather structurally indissociable, from something like a nuclear *epoch* (by nuclear "epoch", I also mean the *épochè* suspending judgment before the absolute decision)."[14] Here, as Ruthven points out, Derrida is playing on the etymological root of the word epoch, in the Greek *epokhe* meaning stoppage. Hence Derrida is not merely referring to the nuclear epoch as merely one stage in historical progression, but at the epoch, which marks the end of such a progression.[15] Although, 'end' is a loaded word with perhaps too many connotations to Fukuyama's 'end of history' discussed above. Derrida's conception of the *épochè* is much more delicate and he himself rejects this Hegelian conception of the end of history. He writes:

> The nuclear age is not an epoch, it is the absolute *épochè*; it is not absolute knowledge and the end of history, it is the *épochè* of absolute knowledge. Literature belongs to this nuclear epoch, that of the crisis and of nuclear criticism, at least if we mean by this the historical and ahistorical horizon of an absolute self-destructibility without apocalypse, without revelation of its own truth, without absolute knowledge.[16]

This is the suspension of 'truth' as absolute knowledge - apocalypse means revelation of truth. There will be no end of history due to an understanding of absolute truth; especially not in the clumsy way which Fukuyama sees absolute truth as liberal democracy. Rather, the very possibility of absolute truth is blocked by the historical and ahistorical (because it has not yet taken place) horizon of nuclear war. What remains in the present, remains before the event of remainderless destruction, is the epoch of literature.

Hence literature becomes vitally important to the nuclear age, and vice versa the nuclear age becomes vitally important to literature, in fact even essential. This relationship announces the fundamental nature of literature. Derrida writes:

> In what I am calling in another sense an absolute epoch, literature comes to life and can only experience its own precariousness, its death menace and its essential finitude. The movement of inscription is the very possibility of its effacement. Thus one cannot be satisfied with saying that, in order to become serious and interesting today, a literature and a literary criticism must refer to the nuclear issue, must even be obsessed by it. That has to be said, and it is true. But I believe also that, at least indirectly, they have always done this. Literature has always belonged to the nuclear epoch, even if it does not talk "seriously" about it.[17]

Literature comes to life when faced with its own death; this means it must be fascinated by this possibility. This does not necessarily mean that literature must always be about nuclear war explicitly. Derrida states that he thinks that the works of Joyce, Mallarmé and Kafka all deal with the nuclear epoch more "seriously" than works about "real" nuclear war. This is because these texts - Joyce, Mallarmé and Kafka - are all part of the deconstructive movement of nuclear literature: The way in which they deal with the possibility of their own death, the death of literature. This is the way in which literature deconstructs itself via its confrontation with its own essential finitude.

This is another interesting point of comparison between nuclear criticism and futurism. Marinetti also put forward a program of experimental literature in a series of manifestos. His aim was to destroy 'traditional' literature by a process of grammatical and linguistic experimentation. While Derrida points towards actual outcomes for literature, the explicit discussion of such outcomes will come later, after the full expression of the aporia of the nuclear referent. The result of this essential marriage of literature and nuclear war is the first version of the paradox of the referent. Derrida expresses this in two points:

1. Literature belongs to the nuclear age by virtue of the performative character of its relation to the referent, and the structure of the written archive. 2. Nuclear war has not taken place, it is a speculation, an invention in the sense of a fable or an invention to be invented in order to make a place for it or to prevent it from taking place (as much invention is needed for one as for the other), and for the moment all this is only literature. Some might conclude that therefore it is not real, as it remains entirely suspended in its fabulous and literary *épochè*.[18]

The first point concerns the necessary relationship between literature and the possibility of nuclear war as the destruction of the archive. Literature is dependent upon the juridico-literary archive, and understanding of literature, the very job of the critic, only becomes possible as a result of the idea of completeness which the end of the archive, that is, its destruction by total nuclear war. As a result, on one side the possibility of criticism is the very nature of nuclear criticism; and on the other, literature exists as the deconstruction of its own possibility, that is the performative action of its own self-reference. This is made more explicit by the second point, which refers to the textual nature of nuclear war. Nuclear war itself is a textual fiction, that is, it is literature. Hence, the literature of nuclear war is literature *par excellence*. However, because it can never refer beyond itself and its own possibility it cannot be 'real', and cannot get beyond its own fabulous *épochè*. Here the self-referential nature of nuclear criticism begins to explode. This leads to the second formulation of the aporia of the nuclear referent, its totality.

The central contention of the aporia of the nuclear referent is the idea that at the same time its conditions of possibility are also

27

its conditions of impossibility. Because literature is conditioned by the stockpile of the archive and because it is only possible to conceive of this archive in its totality because of the threat of its total destruction, then literature itself is conditioned by the fable of total destruction. However, because total destruction has not taken place, it itself is only possible in literature. This means that the referent of any possible literature is intimately connected to its own fictional destruction, all literary reference, and hence all nuclear reference is an absolute fabrication, there can be no nuclear referent other than its own self-reference. The converse side of this is that while there is no "real" referent of any nuclear discourse, this means that all reference is real and there can be no other possible reference/referent. Derrida writes:

> If we are bound and determined to speak in terms of reference, nuclear war is the only possible referent of any discourse and any experience would share their condition with that of literature. If, according to a structuring hypothesis, a fantasy or phantasm, nuclear war is equivalent to the total destruction of the archive, if not of the human habitat, it becomes the absolute referent, the horizon and condition of all others.[19]

Because the only way to engage with the essence of literature is to talk of its destruction, which can only take place in literature, the self-reference of this nuclear referent is the only real referent possible, i.e., the only one which contends with its own conditions of possibility. As such, it is the totality of the nuclear referent that makes any literary reference possible. Hence, the nuclear referent is the absolute referent of all possible reference; yet at the same time it is the destruction of all possible literature. This is the aporia of the nuclear referent.

Derrida highlights the significance of this aporia by contrasting symbolic nature of the total destruction of nuclear war with the relatively minor destruction of the death of an individual. An individual death is intricately connected to the symbolic work of mourning and monumentalization.[20] This work of memory, or remembrance, which works on the remainder of society, is important because of the way in which it softens the "reality" of death by placing it in the realm of the symbolic. This is a particular function of literature, both in the way in which the death of an individual can be represented in advance and the way in which it can be mourned in retrospect, which is defined by the function of the symbolic (or reference).[21] The nuclear issue reverses this process of remembrance and monumentalization. This is exactly the point made by the J.G. Ballard quote that is an epigraph to this book. Because there is no after of the nuclear catastrophe the temporal logic of remembrance must be reversed and the monument must beckon the disaster which will destroy not create it, the stress is always pre-traumatic, not post-traumatic. The total nuclear war will irreversibly destroy the entire archive, and with it all symbolic capacity. There will be no possible memorial because the very possibility of the symbolic itself will be destroyed. A memorial always requires a survival, which it the very symbolic nature of the monument, it is always to that which survives not that which dies. The nature of this symbolic gesture is reversed by the aporia of the nuclear referent. Derrida writes:

> This absolute referent of all possible literature is on par with the absolute effacement of any possible trace; it is thus the only ineffaceable trace, it is so as the trace of what is entirely other, *"trace du tout autre."* This is the only absolute trace - effaceable, ineffaceable. The only "subject" of all possible literature, of all possible criticism, its only ultimate and a-symbolic referent, unsymbolisable, even unsignifiable; this is, if not the nuclear age, if not the nuclear catastrophe, at least that toward which nuclear discourse and the nuclear

29

symbolic *are still beckoning*: the remainderless and a-symbolic destruction of literature.[22]

Here is the aporia of the nuclear referent in all its deconstructive splendor: Firstly, it represents both the destruction of the trace and the absolute possibility of the trace. This is the double movement of all writing, the effacement of all previous writing and the necessity of that same writing. Or, to use the deconstructive terms, the differing and the deferral that together make up *différance*.[23] Secondly is the explicitly futural nature of the nuclear referent. The only possible "subject" of literature, the absolute referent, which holds literature in its epochal suspension, is still beckoning from the future. It is this future as futural, which makes possible all literature; the still beckoning of remainderless destruction, which can be none other than the future perfect.

It is through an understanding of the aporia of the nuclear referent that nuclear criticism is able to rethink the future in terms of the future perfect and hence confront the problem of the (non) event of 1984. Instead of considering the utopian future anterior of *1984*, if 1984 is thought in terms of the epochal suspension of the aporia of the nuclear referent then the (non) event is no longer problematic, because the event has no longer not happened, but is merely suspended. It is in this sense that it was possible to say at the start of the book that the beginning of the future will have been in 1984. This is the beginning of the future perfect, which is held is epochal suspension by the aporia of the nuclear referent, a suspension which is always futural. In many ways this point has added nothing to the above discussion on the future and the (non) event of 1984. However, what must be remembered is the other important event of 1984 discussed above; that is, the end of art. Several similarities between the discourse of nuclear criticism and the artistic movement of futurism have already been defined. The most important of these is the connection between the destruction of history and the production of something new and futural. This points towards a second important development in the conjunction of 1984. The way in which by synthesizing the two futural discourses of nuclear criticism and futurism a new idea of the avant-garde as some sort of nuclear futurism may overcome the idea of the end of art. The way in which this is possible is by examining the various consequences which Derrida draws from his discussion of the aporia of the nuclear referent, the synthesizing these with various elements of futurism in order to critique criticism itself, literature, art, the avant-garde and the end of art.

The most immediate consequences of the aporia of the nuclear referent stem directly from the second formulation of the aporia: the idea of the absolute referent. Because literature and literary criticism can speak of nothing else apart from the nuclear referent, the only thing that they can do is multiply and invent their strategic maneuvers in an attempt to assimilate the wholly other of the absolute trace. This is most obvious as the sort of 'double talk' and rhetoric that defines the diplomatic strategy of nuclear politics.[24] Such as the ideas of the strategic use of nuclear weapons, the rhetorical discussion of 'prevailing' in a nuclear war, and, most specifically and with the most deconstructive overtones, the idea of deterrence, which is a sort of deferral. Alongside this practical outcome is a much more philosophical one. The absolute "subject" of the nuclear referent is an unnamable one, and the same goes for the referent itself. This means that the perspective of nuclear war, and the discourse of nuclear criticism, re-elaborates the very question of the referent itself - what is a referent? Derrida directly connects this re-elaboration of the question of the referent with a simultaneous re-elaboration of the question of the transcendental ego or transcendental subject.[25] This connection seems to stem from the equivocation of the word "subject" as both subject of the discourse and the discourse of subjectivity. This correlation becomes much more apparent in the seventh missile/missive where Derrida plays on another equivocation, this time between nuclear criticism and Kantian criticism. He writes

> "Nuclear criticism", like Kantian criticism, is thought about the limits of experience as a thought of finitude. The *intuitus derivativus* of the receptive (that is, perceiving) being, of which the human subject is only one example, cuts its figure on the (back)ground of the *intuitus originarius*, of an infinite intellect which creates its own objects rather than inventing them.[26]

The nature of both forms of critique is an exploration of conditions of possibility as thoughts of limit or finitude. Kantian criticism is concerned with the possibility of the human subject, whereas nuclear criticism is concerned with the subject of reference. However, considering these two forms of criticism together highlights the problems of Kantian criticism when its subject, the human subject, is conflated with the subject of nuclear criticism. Nuclear criticism reveals that the conditions of possibility of the nuclear referent, and hence all reference in general, are also their own conditions of impossibility. The result of this is that nuclear criticism

> forecloses a finitude so radical that it would annul the basis of the opposition and would make it possible to think the very limit of criticism. This limit comes into view in the groundlessness of a remainderless self-destruction of the self, autodestruction of the *autos* itself. Whereupon the kernel, the nucleus of criticism, itself bursts apart.[27]

There are two pertinent points here. The first is that when this logic of nuclear criticism is applied back to Kantian criticism, that which is destroyed by this self-destruction is exactly the self as the transcendental subject, the subject capable of self-reflectivity.

The destruction of the *autos* itself disrupts the possibility of autonomy and apperception, which together ground the Kantian subject, although it must be said in a mysterious and not entirely unproblematic way to start. This is the kernel of Kantian criticism. The second point is the consequences which this has for criticism, for the self-destruction of the self that is criticism is also its own self-destruction, the nucleus of criticism, its very possibility, is destroyed. The bursting apart of the kernel of criticism is also the explosion of philosophy. This is in many ways the apocalypse of philosophy that can never arrive, which is always held in epochal suspension. However, what remains in the present is the proliferation and invention of strategic maneuvers which prefigure this apocalypse; that is, philosophy in an apocalyptic tone. Although Derrida explores this point in more detail elsewhere,[28] it is this point which he concludes with via the biblical reference of the war of the name and the writing of the apocalypse.[29]

The concept of philosophy as the apocalyptic foreshadowing of its own destruction seems to go against the futural nature of the conclusions already drawn from the aporia of the nuclear referent. With regard to philosophy, in his sixth missile/missive Derrida presents a quite different set of corollaries to the aporia of the nuclear referent. Rather than focusing on Kantian criticism and its relation to nuclear criticism, these set of corollaries are based around the Heideggerian formulation of the essence of metaphysics: namely, the question 'why is there something rather than nothing?'[30] For Heidegger this question - the question of metaphysics - is the primary concern of philosophy, and as such is the search for ground. This philosophical task is, for Heidegger, an extended elaboration on the logic of the ontico-ontological difference. The ontico-ontological difference was exactly where Derrida's nuclear criticism started, with, 'at the beginning there will have been speed'. The speed of nuclear criticism both unites the two elements of the ontico-ontological difference and also, by echoing Genesis, echoes the explicitly Heideggerian investigation into origins and essences. The Heideggerian interpretation of the corollaries of nuclear criticism is expressed when Derrida writes:

> If the ontico-ontological difference ensures the gathering up of the sending (*le rassemblement de cet envoi*), the dissemination and destinerrance I am talking about go so far as to suspend that ontico-ontological difference itself.[31]

The important move at work here is the introduction of the idea of sending or giving, an idea that has been implicit within Derrida's paper all along in the idea of missivity. These interconnected ideas of sending and giving are significant elements of Heidegger's later work. This has particular relevance to the way in which he considers the future of thought. For example both 'The Question Concerning Technology' and 'The End of Philosophy and The Task of Thinking' conclude with a sending or giving forth into thought that signal a path for thinking to take.[32] Derrida takes up this idea in the form of *envoi*, which is sending or a dispatch, and the associated destinerrance (a wandering of its own end). The flip side of this is the idea of gathering, which, for Heidegger, is the task of philosophy, and is more commonly termed bringing to presence (although the bringing of this gathering is just as important as the eventual presence). This gathering is always watched over by the ontico-ontological difference and the search for ground. Derrida's contention is that the radical speed of the nuclear missile/missive results in both a sending and a destinerrance, which will suspend the onticoontological difference.

These two sides, the gathering and the sending, are codependant upon one another. This means that the 'Kantian' interpretation cannot be dismissed, the destinerrance will in some sense always be apocalyptic; philosophy will be trapped wandering within the limits of the ontico-ontological difference. However, by activating the Heideggerian motif of the sending there is the possibility of a path beyond critique. The shape of this path is the speeding missile, the missivity of nuclear criticism, which explosively strikes at the ground zero of literature and philosophy. Derrida writes:

> Just as all language, all writing, every poetico-performative or theoretico-informative text dispatches, sends itself, allows itself to be sent, so today's missiles, whatever their underpinnings may be, allow themselves to be described more readily than ever as dispatches in writing (code, inscription, trace, and so on). That does not reduce them to the dull inoffensiveness that some would naively attribute to books. It recalls (exposes, explodes) that which, in writing, always includes the power of the death machine.[33]

This speeding missile can be none other than literature; but note, it is a literature that has expanded and engulfed every gesture, every maneuver, into the text of writing, specifically the poetico-performative discourse of art and the theoretico-informative discourse of science. All of this, all literature, is watched over by death. What is of importance here is not the drawing out of the proximity of the essence of literature with death, but the way in which, as a result or outcome of this, the sending of the text always includes the power of the death machine, and that a text will always send forth this machine of death. The connections between death, literature, writing and philosophy are central to the philosophy of Derrida, and themes that he has approached from a variety of angles, and yet which all together underpin all of his work.

Chapter 4

The End of the Book and the Beginning of Writing

Although this particular text 'No Apocalypse, Not Now' is a relatively minor one in Derrida's *oeuvre* this injunction towards experimental literature and the way in which it is structured with respect to the writing of philosophy, *envoi*, the future, and both death and the death machine, opens another reading of Derrida's work as a whole. The first important point here is that all of Derrida's work, from *Of Grammatology* onwards, may be understood as a calling for, and also a sending of - this connection will be developed below - experimental writing and literature. It is the affinity between the nuclear epoch, literature and deconstruction that motivates Derrida's explicit call to experimental literature. Although here this link is explored from within the context of the aporia of the nuclear referent, the mobilization of the important Derridean concept of deconstruction, a concept which is often seen as his major philosophical point, indicates that the links between deconstruction and experimental literature which are explicitly stated here appear, or at least are implicit within other areas of Derrida's work. Just as the nuclear epoch is a suspension of truth or the impossibility of absolute knowledge, what the deconstructive process does is reveal the way in which truth, and in particular metaphysical determinations of truth, is always inseparable from the logos.[1] This logocentric manifestation of truth is based around the determination "of the being of the entity as presence."[2] The result of this logocentric determination of truth is that writing, as a sort of absence that appears as the difference between signified and signifier, is considered to be detached from the truth of presence. Derrida's project is structured around these two concepts and the various outcomes of their aporetic interaction. Stated as such there are two questions or observations that are immediately evident. Firstly, how does the all important interaction function and in what ways is it apparent, or how is it made apparent and via what process? The second is the concept of outcomes, which in a sense betrays an important element of Derrida's work that has already been examined thoroughly, that is its futural dimension. We must remember that these two lines of questioning are themselves co-dependant and interactive.

The first question, that of methods of recognizing and engaging with logocentrism and its manifestations, gives rise to the Derridean concept of deconstruction and the numerous related conceptual devices and tools he uses. Deconstruction is a method of philosophy that is first and foremost a way of engaging with philosophy as a set of texts and the written word. It is here that the central aporia functions. How is it possible for the essential presence of logocentrism to be expressed in a text, which is a debased form of discourse due to the absence of the detachment of the signifier? The answer Derrida gives is that philosophy has functioned via the metaphor of the book. What the book represents is a totality, which refers to the natural totality philosophy is continually searching for, the totality of the logos.[3] Hence Derrida's understanding of writing allows a line of engagement with, and attack against the entire domain of philosophy constituted as a book. He writes:

> The idea of the book, which always refers to a natural totality, is profoundly alien to the sense of writing. It is the encyclopaedic protection of theology and of logocentrism against its aphoristic energy, and ... difference in general. If I distinguish the text from the book, I shall say that the destruction of the book, as is now under way in all domains, denudes the surface of the text. That necessary violence responds to a violence that was no less necessary.[4]

The book functions as a logocentric protective metaphor against the anarchic absence of writing. The power of this metaphor derives from two sources: Firstly, the theological idea of the divine text as the word of God; and, secondly, the metaphysical idea of the natural law, or writing of nature, which legitimizes the task of metaphysics. By appealing to the both the book of God and the book of nature there is an implicit move towards the unity of the logos defining philosophy. Hence, Derrida's deconstructive method is the violent reading of the text as writing against the metaphyscio-theological roots of the book and thus against logocentrism itself. Derrida develops a rigorous science of writing - grammatology - which specifies the various devices and methods by which such violent deconstructive readings operate.[5] These devices are elaborated throughout his work as a complex set of concepts that allow texts to be read in many different ways. They include *différance*, play, the *grammè*, the supplement, *écart* and the trace. Of these, the last - the trace - is the most important and the most interesting because of the way in which it has implications for the historicist element of Derrida's work.

The trace is central to the science of grammatology because it is both a method of examining a text and that which is at the essence of all texts. It can thus be considered much like the method of phenomenology whereby phenomena are analyzed in order to ascertain their origin, essence, or conditions of possibility. First and foremost the trace is the violent inscription of the text, the actual writing traced upon the page. It is this which gives grammatology its most concrete content, the *grammè* - the written mark, the word - from the Greek *gramma* meaning letter or writing.[6] It must be noted that the concept of the *grammè* as the content of grammatology also contains the concept of trace in all its conceptions. The historical determinations of the *grammè* are made clear in the way in which it serves as a technology - *techne* - of liberated memory as language moves from the spoken to written word. This liberation of memory also gave a linearity to the concept of time, which in turn is central to historical thought.[7] However, considering the *grammè* as the possibility of history also raises the need to think the history of the *grammè*. This is the next level of the idea of the trace: the historical trace that runs through all texts. This is the violent residue of all writing, the collected historical determinations of each *grammè*, which, due to the nature of the written word, remains as an inscription, which may be used to trace each and every instance and use of that word. What is important for Derrida in using this aspect of the trace as part of his grammatological method is how it reveals that writing functions by an originary difference rather than synthesis. That is, it is the difference between each use of a word, which makes meaning possible rather than a primary synthesis or simplicity of all such uses. This in turn exposes what Derrida calls the pure trace, he writes:

> Here the appearing and functioning of difference presup-
> poses an originary synthesis not preceded by absolute
> simplicity. Such would be the originary trace. Without
> retention in the minimal unit of temporal experience, without
> a trace retaining the other as other in the same, no difference
> would do its work and no meaning would appear. It is not a
> question of constituted difference here, but rather, before all
> determination of the content, of the *pure* movement which
> produced difference. *The (pure) trace is différance.* It does not
> depend on any sensible plenitude, audible or visible, phonic
> or graphic. It is, on the contrary, the condition of such a
> plenitude.[8]

Here Derrida introduces another grammatological concept, that of *différance*, the neologism created by combining the two ideas of differ and defer, which share a common origin in the Latin *differre* and appear in the French *différer*.[9] *Différance* is a complex notion that functions at several levels. In one sense it is the method utilized in any reading, which Derrida mobilizes as part of the phenomenological like toolbox of the science of grammatology: The differentiation of the word from all others and the deferral of understanding the full context of the reading. In another sense this is the very possibility of any, indeed many, understandings, and yet at the same time the impossibility of a full or singular understanding that must always be deferred. Hence, it is by the operation of *différance* in the reading of a text that the trace in all reading appears. As Derrida says above, the pure trace is *différance*.

The dual structure of *différance* as differing and deferring relates to the dual structures of space and time at work in writing. The differences of these two dimensions - spatial and temporal - are evident in that they function both as retention and protention: As the differences of the retention of the past and as the production of the deferred differences of the future. Both of these functions are clearly at odds with the logocentric preference for a metaphysics of presence. Indeed, a logocentric metaphysics of time which seeks to subsume the past and the future under the present as either past-present or future-present, is incapable of adequately describing the structure of the trace.[10] The critique of the metaphysics of time in terms of presence is very similar to the one that has taken place above in terms of the future anterior. Here the future-present is the same as the future anterior, it is the very anteriority of the future anterior which allows it to be conceived as present. At the very start of *Of Grammatology* Derrida has already foreshadowed the problematization of the future anterior when he writes:

The future can only be anticipated in the form of an absolute danger. It is that which breaks absolutely with constituted normality and can only be proclaimed, *presented*, as a sort of monstrosity. For that future world and for that within it which will have put into question the values of sign, word, and writing for that which guides out future anterior, there is yet no exergue.[11]

This whole statement effectively pre-empts the entire domain of nuclear criticism, in its absolute danger, and its outcomes for temporality, spatiality and ontology in general; and also shows the way in which the relatively minor text of 'No Apocalypse, No Now' is a vital element of Derrida's work, as it begins to present a thinking of this absolute danger as a potential positive guide beyond it, that is, towards the future whatever that may be.

While the trace problematizes the logocentric metaphysics of time the very act of calling the future into question produces its own logic of temporality rooted in Derrida's analysis of writing. The name Derrida gives to this device is spacing and its relation to the trace is clear in the French word *écart*. The trace itself is not a metaphysical entity, but rather a mechanism whereby the discourse of metaphysics, in its very conditions of possibility, is called into question. Likewise, spacing is not another metaphysical device put in the place cleared by the trace. Rather the two devices work in tandem both within and upon the writing of metaphysics. If the trace is a deconstructive reading process, which exposes *différance* and deconstructs logocentrism; then spacing is a reconstructive writing, which is always becoming and moving beyond the present text and the text of presence. Derrida writes:

Spacing (notice this word speaks the articulation of space and time, the becoming-space of time and the becoming-time of space) is always unperceived, the nonpresent, and the nonconscious. *As such*, if one can still use that expression in a non-phenomenological way; for here we pass the very limits of phenomenology. Arche-writing as spacing cannot occur *as such* within the phenomenological experience of *presence*. It marks the *dead time* within the presence of the living present, within the general form of all presence. The dead time is at work. That is why, once again, in spite of all the discursive resources that the former may borrow from the latter, the concept of the trace will never be merged with a phenomenology of writing. As the phenomenology of the sign in general, a phenomenology of writing is impossible. No intuition can be realized in the place where "the 'whites' indeed take on an importance."[12]

Here Derrida constructs spacing as that which is hidden in all writing and which will be exposed by the trace. However, such exposure is not part of a phenomenology of writing although it often utilizes the phenomenological method. Spacing is the putting to work of this hidden element, an element that by its very nature must remain hidden, the dead time. This working dead time alludes both to the death machine of experimental literature and also to the place of death within phenomenological philosophy. Derrida expands upon this latter point when he states that:

As the subject's relationship with its own death, this becoming [the becoming-absent of spacing] is the constitution of subjectivity. On all levels of life's organization, that is to say, of *the economy of death*.[13]

The aporia of death as the condition of possibility of subjectivity makes an important appearance here within Derrida's analysis of writing. This indicates more general points of interaction between what might be called Derrida's linguistic philosophy and philosophy in general. As will be further developed throughout the rest of this book, this exposes the way in which nuclear futurism as a sort of experimental writing will deal with the central issues of the problem of future futurity as a problem for philosophy in general. Spacing is connected explicitly to experimental literature, and also with the impossibility of a phenomenology of writing, by the invocation of Mallarmé who may be considered the father of modern experimental literature. This is through the reference to the importance of the 'whites' or the particular organizational spacing on the page central to Mallarmé's poetry.

As with all Derridian terms spacing operates in many different ways. It is the opening up of a deferred time within which the play of difference appears, a future writing that is beyond the logocentric domination of metaphysics. Yet, it is also already within the writing of metaphysics waiting to be exposed by the trace, an exposure which produces a becoming, a new writing. It is also part of the very method of such new writing, an experimental product of the death machine which itself operates as a space of absence within the metaphysical discourse. Spacing cannot be separated from the trace. Like their own written words - trace-*écart* - they are mirror images of each other. The trace deconstructs, exposing absence within the various writings of logocentrism, while spacing is the hiddenness of this absence and also its becoming, a writing which has, and always must be deferred, and yet which is always coming. At the center of this dual operation is the text being deconstructed. The encounter between the trace and spacing is then a hinge which bends the text out of joint - deconstructs - or, as Derrida puts it: "The hinge [*brisure*] marks the impossibility that a sign, the unity of a signifier and a signified, be produced within the plenitude of a present and an absolute presence."[14] In its temporal character-istic, the present as an absolute presence, this hinge is the 'time out of joint' that Hamlet observes and which is central to Derrida's analysis of Marx in *Specters of Marx*, and which is indicative of the problem of future futurity.

Chapter 5

Spectral Matters

The hinge that is out of joint, that it is necessary to be set right by Hamlet through the double movement of trace and *écart*, returns to the very nature of the aporia in general as well as the aporias of subjectivity and death. Thus the hinge unites the critique of temporality as future futurity – the time is out of joint – with the logic of hauntology and the fundamental nature of the aporia in general. The logic of the aporia is already one of the joint, the border and the possibilities and problems of any beyond. In the book *Aporias: Dying - awaiting (one another at) the "limits of truth"* Derrida describes it as:

> There, in sum, is this place of the aporia, *there is no longer any problem.* Not that, alas or fortunately, the solutions have been given, but because one could no longer even find a problem that would constitute itself and that one would keep in front of oneself, as a presentable object or project, as a protective representative or a prosthetic substitute, as some kind of border to cross or behind which to protect oneself.[1]

While the aporia seems to represent a typical philosophical problem it is very different from the usual sort of dialectical argumentation of thesis and antithesis. Rather the aporia is somewhat paradoxical in that the way that it determines a problem is such that the problem cannot be resolved by any passage beyond it, as the very possibility of such passage would negate the existence of the aporia in the first place. Just as the aporia of the nuclear referent ceases to exist in the case of any 'real' nuclear war and thus is only held in possibility by the impossibility of its own eventuality. Importantly, this has consequences for temporality in the (de)construction of borders and beyond suggested by the logic of the aporia.

The aporia does not function by opposing one thing, object or beyond against another one present or here. Just as the future of a future futurity is not another complete time as it is with the future anterior. The function of the aporia is not one of opposition or contrast, as Derrida writes: "the partitioning [*partage*] among multiple figures of the aporia does not oppose figures to each other, but instead installs the haunting of one in the other."[2] Thus, as something that cannot be resolved but must be experienced, the logic of the aporia appears as a logic of haunting, or a hauntology, which disrupts its homophone ontology. Although he does not coin the term hauntology until *Specters of Marx*, the logic of haunting that it describes is already at work in *Aporias*. Indeed *Aporias* may be read itself as a hinge in Derrida's work. In a uncharacteristic passage on pages 15 and 16 Derrida traces the way that the logic of the aporia, as what he calls "aporetology or aporetography"[3] has been the underlying struggle of much of his previous work, including important texts such as *Glas, Margins of Philosophy* and *Limited Inc. Aporias* first appeared as a conference address in July 1992,[4] just under a year later in April 1993, in the lectures that form the foundation of *Specters of Marx*, the logic of the aporia reappears as hauntology, with the more ethical and political focus characteristic of Derrida's later works.

Although unnamed as such, hauntology and the specter are already beginning to appear in the work done in *Aporias* and thus this work is in many ways provides important context and indeed grounding for the later and fuller account of the ghost in *Specters of Marx*. Derrida recognizes this himself. In sketching out the corollaries of the argument put forward in *Aporias* he says:

In an economic, elliptic, hence dogmatic way, I would say that there is no politics without an organization of time and space of mourning, without a topoliology of the sepulcher, without an anamnesic and thematic relation to the spirit as ghost [*revenant*], without an open hospitality to the guest as *ghost* [in English in the original], whom one holds, just as he holds us, hostage.[5]

What is elliptic and dogmatic in *Aporias* emerges in its fuller form in *Specters of Marx* where Derrida, in setting out the project of the book, states:

It is necessary to speak *of the* ghost, indeed *to the* ghost and *with* it, from the moment that no ethics, no politics, whether revolutionary or not, seems possible and thinkable and *just* that does not recognize in its principle the respect for those others who are not yet *there*, presently living, whether they are dead or not yet born.[6]

In that the ghost becomes central to Derrida's thought on the political, it also become vital to the philosophy of the future. In *Specters of Marx* Derrida explicitly addresses the problem of the collapse of the Soviet Union, the declaration of the end of history, and the question of the future of Marxism, and it is this question that prompts the wider question of the possibility of the political in general, and raises the issues of the ghost. On this question Derrida writes: "This question *arrives*, if it arrives, it questions with regard to what will come in the future-to-come. Turned toward the future, going toward it, it also comes from it, it proceeds *from* [*provident* de] the future."[7] All of which reveals the way in which the ghost problematizes and disrupts the notions of time and the future in a way that is particularly pertinent to the issues of future futurity and also shows how this issue is itself in turn fundamental to questions of politics and ethics. The important connection that Derrida has made here is between politics as justice and the necessity of justice to extend beyond the living present in a way heralding another entrance of the ghost. He writes:

> To be just: beyond the living present in general – and beyond its simple negative reversal. A spectral moment, a moment that no longer belongs to time, if one understands by this word the linking of modalized presents (past present, actual present: "now," future present) ... Furtive and untimely, the apparition of the specter does not belong to that time[8]

The spectral moment, the question of politics as justice beyond the living present, itself conjures up the specter and in doing so disrupts time and the possibilities of the future. This returns to the fundamental question that initially revealed, or compelled the apparition of, the specter in *Aporias*, that is, the possibility of a 'beyond the living present.'

Aporias commences with the question: "Is my death possible?"[9] and once again is echoed by *Specters of Marx*, which starts with the statement "I would like to learn to live finally."[10] Between these two statements the similarities relating the aporia of the nuclear referent and the subject of death begin to appear. Just as the impossibly textual possibility of total destruction determines the conditions of possibility of literature, so too does death become important in establishing the impossible conditions of possibility for the subject. It is the finality of death that makes the living of life possible in this latter statement, but as the former asks, is it even possible to think that finally as 'my death'? This conjunction of death and finality returns to the more general question of ends and by extension to that of borders, and hence to aporia as a boundary but not a border. The distinction between death and ends is a vital element of Heidegger's investigation into death, which is central to *Being and Time*. This distinction also answers the question about 'my death.' Heidegger writes:

No one can take the Other's dying away from him. Of course someone can 'go to his death for another'. But that always means to sacrifice oneself for the Other '*in some definite affair*'. Such "dying for" can never signify that the Other has thus had his death taken away in even the slightest degree. ... By its very essence, death is in every case mine, in so far as it 'is' at all.[11]

For Heidegger the mine-ness of death is essential to death itself, and vice versa death is essential to the mine-ness of subjectivity. This is why it is important for Heidegger to make a distinction between death, as dying properly (the etymological relationship between mine or own and proper will become important in Chapter 7 with regards to Heidegger's conception of the event) and ends. Death is distinct from other ends, ending or *telos* such as ripeness or maturity, as these limits or ends are not necessary for death; indeed, with regard to them death always comes too soon or too late.

It is this distinction that allows Heidegger to situate what he calls his existential analysis of death before any 'metaphysics of death' and before all biology,[12] the discourses of which would never be enough to account for the mine-ness of death. The result is that:

Heidegger thus suggests an ontological delimitation among the fields of inquiry concerning death. This delimitation seems all the more abyssal because it concerns limits about the questions of the limit, more precisely, questions of ends, of the modes of ending, and of the limit that separates simple *ending* from *properly dying*.[13]

It is this ontological delimitation, which functions through the ontico-ontological difference that Heidegger seeks to undercut, that prompts Derrida's plea for the ghost as the ground of the political. Derrida plays with many limits and borders in the short text of *Aporias*, but this de-cision, drawn along the ontico-ontological difference between the existential analytic of death as such, in all its irreducible mine-ness, and other sorts of ends such as perishing, that is the most important border at work. To reduce death to the existential analytic as Heidegger does means that there is no way to think death properly in any ontic or specific terms. At the same time death has no border as it is foundational to all beings in terms of the existential analytic, and yet this also means that culture and different cultures cannot engage with death as such. Death extends everywhere and yet at the same time remains neutral with regards to each area it extends into. These are the first two corollaries that Derrida draws from the aporia of Heidegger's existential analysis of death.[14] The third corollary is the consequences that this might have for politics in the sense that if there can be no political engagement with death, then by Derrida's argument there can be no politics at all, as all politics depends upon the ghost as guest and the logic of mourning, remembrance and memorialization.[15]

The determination of the ghost as guest reveals two other important elements of Derrida's examination of death in *Aporias*, as well as pointing towards the extended development of hauntology in *Specters of Marx*. These are both organized around the thinking of death itself as a limit or border. This is itself a reiteration of Heidegger's famous definition of death as "the possibility of the absolute impossibility for *Dasein*."[16] Without going too far into the particularities and peculiarities of *Dasein*, except to say that it is the being that understands, or at least stands in relation to it own Being and thus bridges the ontico-ontological difference; this is almost the most fundamental statement regarding the possibility of *Dasein* that Heidegger makes. It is through death as such, dying properly, or being-towards-death that *Dasein* is aware of its own finitude and the very there-ness of its Being. As Heidegger puts it: "With death,

Dasein stands before itself in its ownmost potentiality-for-being."[17] Derrida's reiteration of this highlights the temporal element at work here: "With death *Dasein* is indeed *in front of* itself *(bevor)*, both as before a mirror and as before the future: it awaits itself [*s'attend*], it precedes itself [*se précède*], it has a rendezvous with itself."[18] Death is futural in that it is always to-come and must always be awaited and yet can never arrive, and as such it follows the logic of the aporia: The impossibility of living ones death is the very limit of the possibility of both living and death.[19]

Here then are the two elements: death as an uncrossable and aporetic *border or limit* that can only be *awaited*. Derrida writes: "It is on this border that I am tempted to read Heidegger. Yet this border will always keep one from discriminating among the figures of the *arrivant*, the dead, and the *revenant* (the ghost, he, she, or that which returns)."[20] This returns to the third corollary and the limiting problem of the limits of the existential analysis of death. Likewise, this also returns to the spectral absent others and the entire project of *Specters of Marx*; and also to the fundamental distinction that Heidegger makes when he says that it is impossible to die for the other. This is the limit that Derrida speaks of when he says: "The relevance of the question of knowing whether it is from one's own proper death or from the other's death that the relation to death or the certitude of death is limited from the start."[21] It is within this aporetic limit of the *arrivant*, the dead, and the *revenant* where the logic of hauntology operates.

Specters of Marx is one of Derrida's most direct, insofar as he is ever direct, engagements with the future. It is the ghosts of the not yet present who provide this futural impulse of questioning and the logic of hauntology in general. This is not merely as some sort of ethical thought experiment or mere injunction of the other. As shown through the ontological grounding done in *Aporias* through Heidegger's existential analytic of death, the ghost cannot help but return as *Dasein* stands before the impossibility its ownmost possibility. The waiting on the aporetic limit of death produces the important distinction between the *revenant* and the *arrivant*. The *arrivant*, as both the arriving and that which arrives, is the condition of being-towards-death, as Derrida explicitly states of it: "the impossible itself, and that this *condition of possibility* of the event [the *arrivant*] is also its *condition of impossibility*"[22] He immediately connects this to a "strange concept of messianism without content, of the messianic without messianism."[23] A vague concept of the future that is somehow not to-come, not future anterior, but a more fundamental force of the futural. This will be explored in more detail in Chapter 11, although it is interesting to note the emergence of the messianic in contrast to the apocalyptic discourse of nuclear criticism.

In the present condition of awaiting the impossible *arrivant* itself what appears in its place is the *revenant*, that which comes back but in this case back from the future. This return sets up the temporal logic of hauntology as the ghost appears not just as a return or repetition of someone once living who is now dead, but as a new emergence of that person from the spectral future of the *arrivant*, Derrida writes:

> Repetition *and* first time: this is perhaps the question of the event as question of the ghost. ... Repetition *and* first time, but also repetition *and* last time, since the singularity of any *first time*, makes it also a *last time*. Each time is the event itself, a first time is a last time. Altogether other. Staging for the end of history. Let us call it a *hauntology*. This logic of haunting would not merely be more powerful than an ontology or a thinking of Being (of the "to be" ...)[24]

There are several important elements in this short section. Importantly the end of history makes an appearance here. The aim of *Specters of Marx* is in once way simple, a critique of

Fukuyama and a rehabilitation of Marx after the end of history. Derrida's deconstruction of the particulars Fukuyama's argument, and the entire 'end of history' type of argument inherited from Kojève is faultless. The analysis of the sleight of hand that allows Fukuyama to declare the empirical triumph of liberal democracy as a 'truth' and at the same time dismiss the possibility of any empirical objection to this truth by mobilization of this truth as 'ideal' completely discredits any philosophical foundation of Fukuyama's position.[25] However, it is telling that despite the simplicity of this deconstruction Derrida must construct hauntology as an entirely new logic of temporality and critique of ontology in order to confront the end of history.

Derrida's aim is much greater than the end of history. As he points out, the theme of ends became so prolific in the fifties that he could identify an apocalyptic tone in philosophy that consisted of "the canon of the modern apocalypse (end of history, end of man, end of Philosophy, Hegel, Marx, Nietzsche, Heidegger, with their Kojèvian codicil and the codicils of Kojève himself [i.e., Fukuyama]."[26] This tone then infects and is reflected by the apocalyptic nature of the world, fist through the barbarity of totalitarianism, but now through a cultural logic of total capitalism, which remains riven with oppression, exploitation and war and where, as pointed out in the Introduction, it is easier to imagine the end of the world than the end of capitalism and thus the contemporary world can only be imagined through the images of the end of the world.[27] In order to confront the total 'out of joint-ness' of this apocalyptic world, Derrida must reconfigure the foundation of the temporality that lead to this apocalyptic condition and disrupt it at it very ontological level. The mechanism that he uses is the logic of hauntology.

Hauntology disrupts ontology in several different ways. The most obvious is the temporal disruption that turns temporality towards the future through the event of the *revenant* as *arrivant*. This return functions through the temporal logic of the first time that is also the last time. This logic has been encountered before; it was the underlying logic of the aporia of the nuclear referent as discussed in Chapter 3, where the absolute inventiveness of the nuclear age prompted this condition. This suggests that the temporality of the specter, that of the first time and the last time and its associated messianism, is connected to the critique of the future anterior and the development of the future perfect. The duality of the messianic and the apocalyptic presents a perfect conceptual schema to confront the out of joint apocalyptic time of ends, through the possibility of a new futurity without end. This critique of temporality and the future plays a role within the wider scope of Derrida's philosophy and the future of philosophy in general, as pointed out by the anticipation of the future as an absolute danger in *Of Grammatology*. This spectral temporality also disrupts the metaphysics of presence that has organized logocentric philosophy, as the ghost is a very obvious example of something that is both present and absent. Derrida describes it as: "The disjointure in the very presence of the present, this non-contemporanity of present time to itself."[28] This closely resembles the temporal structure of the Heideggerian event as something itself critical of temporality and presence, which will be discussed further in Chapter 7.

The disruption of hauntology goes further than the merely temporal. It also contains a much more specific disruption of the ontologies of body, spirit and corporality produced by the ghost. Derrida writes:

the specter is a paradoxical incorporation, the becoming-body, a certain phenomenal and carnal form of the spirit. It becomes, rather, some "thing" that remains difficult to name: neither soul nor body, and both one and the other. For it is flesh and phenomenality that give to the spirit its spectral apparition, but which disappear right away in the apparition, in the very coming of the *revenant* or the return of the specter.[29]

Just as the return of the *revenant* disrupts time by the anachronism of its return, it also disrupts the body, spirit and the phenomenological bridge between the two. This in turn also becomes a critique of the fundamental distinctions between *noesis* and *aethesis*, and phenomena and noumena, which are the foundation of Kantian philosophy. Derrida writes:

> there is no ghost, there is never any becoming-specter of the spirit without at least an appearance of flesh, in a space of invisible visibility, like the dis-appearing of an apparition. For there to be a ghost, there must be a return to the body, but to a body that is more abstract than ever. The spectrogenic process corresponds therefore to a paradoxical *incorporation*. Once ideas or thoughts (*Gedanke*) are detached from their substratum, one engenders some ghost by *giving them a body*.[30]

There is not just a mere indeterminacy between body and spirit, matter and idea or object and concept, but rather an important possibility of relation between them that itself is determined by the specter. This is a fundamental question of metaphysics, hence the appearance of the "thing" in question – the specter – as both a "something" and a "not nothing" of Heidegger's fundamental question of metaphysics. The specter gives a particular answer to this question; it is the materiality on which concepts snag and catch and which is given, and through which is given, experience and knowledge. Ernesto Laclau reads this as an affirmation of transcendence that promotes a sort of politics beyond ideology.[31] However, just as Derrida uses this specter to read Marx's critique of German Idealism in *The German Ideology* as a series of exorcisms of phenomenological ghosts;[32] it is also possible to see here a sort of spectral materialism that echoes Marx's materialist turning of Hegel on his head.

To begin to sketch out this spectral materialism it is necessary to read these two quotes closely and draw out the way in which they both engage with metaphysics and re-engage the possibilities of metaphysics itself. The first important element to point out is the way in which the specter mediates the "thing" as something difficult to name. This returns to the fundamental distinction between ontology and epistemology, or between the questions of what is and how we know what there is. It is not just a question of the nature of reality or being, but also of the mechanism of how knowledge of that reality is possible. Both of these questions condense around the theory of conception as the mechanism whereby thought relates to being. The distinction that this questioning raises between the objects of the world and the concepts used to know those objects is a murky area and it is easy to lose sight of the initial question – what is real? – within the various metaphysical paths and systems set up to deal with this very question.[33] One particular trap is the possibility of this discussion falling into mere questions of meaning or hermeneutics, which dismisses the necessity of any actual object and shifts the question of concepts to one of meaning. All of this is watched over by Kant's Copernican revolution and the fundamental distinction he makes between sensibility and understanding; that is, between the sense data of perception and the classification of an object under a concept.

Derrida's characterization of the ghost as a "thing" that remains difficult to name contains all the elements of this problem. The "thing" is now enclosed in quotes, perhaps quoting Heidegger's *Das Ding*, the thing of phenomenology, or perhaps separating the thingness of the specter from this very thingness of phenomenology. Whichever way it is this "thing" is now haunted by some sort of remains, recalling the physical remains of the body from which the spirit has now departed and the world that it returns to from its past and from the future. The remains and the remainder are that part that cannot be used up, that exceeds understanding, that cannot either be entirely named or subsumed under the concept. That the "thing" remains difficult to name recalls both the epistemological difference between the concept and the word, and also the metaphysical difference between the reality of the concept and the reality of the object as something more than a "thing."

Derrida makes the spectral return to the object explicit in the second quote. The ghost only appears in the distance between the idea or concept and that from which it has been detached, i.e., its object. This distance is the dis- of the disjointed and apart disappearing of the apparition as the appearance of flesh. As Derrida notes, this return is to a body that is more abstract than ever, a process he refers to as "paradoxical incorporation." This is not the epistemologically tinged incorporation of sensibility under a concept, but rather the metaphysical incorporation of the reality of the concept into the reality of the object. The paradoxical nature of this is that the incorporation can only take place through the disappearance of either one or the other. The reality of the flesh of the object is the matter of spectral materialism; however this reality is always different and distant to what can be conceptualized. The reality of the ghost always disappears behind its spectral apparition, and yet in its appearance it is haunted by the loss of that reality, returning to the flesh and giving itself a body.

As with Marx's need to turn Hegel on his head to produce a materialist critique of capitalism, Derrida uses his spectral materialism to develop an alternative ghostly critique of capitalism and reinvigorate Marx's analysis of commodity fetishism. To outline his theory of commodity fetishism as "the mystification of the thing itself"[34] Marx introduces the image of the table made to stand on its head and dance before the market; to present itself no longer as a piece of wood, nor in terms of its use-value, but as an object of the market, perceivable only in its exchange-value. As such, it has abandoned the phenomenological good sense of the object and its perception and is now a sensuous non-sensuous supernatural thing. As Derrida phrases it: "The commodity is a "thing" without phenomenon, a thing in flight that surpasses the senses."[35] The containment of the "thing" within quote marks again indicated that there is another specter present. Indeed, as Derrida notes, it is perhaps not by chance that the image Marx chooses for the commodity is the dancing table, which recalls the movement of the table moved by the ghost in a séance. This allows Derrida to reformulate the commodity in terms of the specter, he writes: "The commodity thus haunts the thing, its specter is at work in use-value."[36] However, like Marx before him, the emphasis placed upon the materiality of the specter provides Derrida with another line to critique the commodity and the enchantments of capitalism. Inversely, it is now the materialism of the specter that haunts the immaterial domain of exchange-value, just as the specter of communism haunts Europe in the opening line of *The Communist Manifesto*. In its very spectral nature the commodity contains the possibility of its own destruction as it demands a return to the flesh, materiality and the distances and spacings of this return.

This metaphysical reading of the dual movement of the specter – the negation of disappearance and the return to the body – recalls the two slopes of literature identified by Maurice Blanchot in 'Literature and the Right to Death.' On the first slope "literature is turned toward the movement of negation by which things a separated from themselves and destroyed in order to be known, subjugated, communicated."[37] While on the second slope:

> Literature is a concern for the reality of things, for their unknown, free, and silent existence; literature is their innocence and their forbidden presence, it is the being which protests against revelation, it is the defiance of what does not want to take place outside. ... it allies itself with the reality of

language, it makes language into matter without contour, content without form[38]

These two slopes of literature, which so closely resemble and reflect Derrida's dual structure of *écart* and trace, also relate to two types of death or negation. The first slope represents the death of thing-as-things as soon as they are translated into objects of knowledge, contemplation or conception through the force of language. Here, then, returns the Kantian distinction between *noesis* and *aethesis* and the establishment of a dialectic of domination through the absolute freedom required to both create and leap across the distance between the object and the concept. Thus for Blanchot, Sade is the writer *par excellence* who both embodies the absolute freedom of the revolution, despite being locked up, and reveals the murderous domination of all language.[39] The second slope of literature is then the attempted negation of this negation, the attempt through language, to return to the thing before it was subjected to language – it is thus the death of language. As the material remains of the reality of the object force the realization that the "thing" remains difficult to name and thus exceeds and demands a return from the subjection of language to the reality of matter. In the unity of literature and its deaths language then becomes "the *life that endures death and maintains itself in it.*"[40] The suspension of the writer and the subject within the ambiguity of these two slopes of literature once again recalls Heidegger's definition of death as the possibility of absolute impossibility, and the question central to *Aporias* 'is my death possible?'[41]

The analysis of *Aporias* formulated this question in relation to self and others; Simon Critchley examines it in terms of suicide;[42] however, Blanchot himself provides another alternative in the story of "a young man prevented from dying by death itself"[43] in 'The Instant of My Death.' The story recounts the wartime experience of a young man, possibly Blanchot himself, who, when placed before a firing squad, feels "extraordinary lightness, a sort of beatitude (nothing happy, however) – sovereign elation? The encounter of death with death?"[44] Only to be reprieved by a nearby explosion upon which he escapes, left only with a changed existence: "As if the death outside of him could only henceforth collide with the death in him. "I am alive. No, you are dead.""[45] Until, in an epilogue set much later, after the end of the war, he recounts: "All that remains is the feeling of lightness that is death itself, or to put it more precisely, the instant of my death henceforth always in abeyance."[46]

'The Instant of my Death' brings together the two slopes of literature, the aporetic limit of death as the possibility of absolute impossibility and the time out of joint of hauntology. The story also provides a link between this last point, the hauntological rupture of temporality, and Derrida's very early work in *Of Grammatology*. This link illuminates that often-overlooked element of the science developed in *Of Grammatology*, the structure of spacing (*écart*). The impossible possibility of death in the story – "I am alive, no you are dead" – appears as an instant that disrupts temporality, that is "henceforth always in abeyance." The instance of the instant, which actually occurred in the past, thus becomes fututral – "henceforth" – and also at the same time, in the same instant, temporally unbound – "always." However, the disjunction of this temporality is also temporarily suspended, it is "in abeyance." While the word "abeyance" most commonly means a state of suspension, its etymology reveals a root in the old French *abeance*, which literally means 'a gaping at.' This gaping is the space opened up by the ruptured temporality of the instant of death as the possibility of the absolute impossible.

Thus the story returns to the concept of *écart*, the spacing or gap of abeyance, opened up in the instant of the possibility of absolute impossibility of death. Temporality is also disjointed in this instant as it reconfigures the "henceforth" and thus the future into a moment of the instant. Now no longer a future futurity, but a future as a gap or absence, already active in the presence of the present; again, the dead time at work in the whites of the *écart*, and the return of the *revenant*. The abeyance of this instant opens up another possibility for the experimental death machine of literature. Firstly, reading back through Blanchot as a writer, but also to encompass the pressing of the present tense in works such as *Ulysses*, Alain Robbe-Grillet's *Jealousy* and Tom McCarthy's *C* (which itself contains a version of the events of Blanchot's story).[47]

'The Instant of my Death' also contains a curious reference to Hegel, which has repercussions for the codicils of the end of history. The section runs:

When the lieutenant returned and became aware the young chatelaine had disappeared, why did anger, rage, not prompt him to burn down the Château (immobile and majestic)? Because it was the Château. On the façade was inscribed, like an indestructible reminder, the date 1807. Was he cultivated enough to know this was the famous year of Jena, when Napoleon, on his small gray horse, passed under the windows of Hegel, who recognized in him the "spirit of the world," as he wrote to a friend? Lie and truth: for as Hegel wrote to another friend, the French pillaged and ransacked his home. But Hegel knew how to distinguish the empirical and the essential.[48]

Here is Hegel, the thinker of the end of history, and his encounter with the world spirit; an end of history nearly two hundred years before Fukuyama's (although as Derrida points out in his analysis of Blanchot, this date is wrong, it should be 1806[49]). Unlike Fukuyama, Hegel is able to distinguish between the empirical and the essential – despite his habit of attributing to 'empirical accident' subjects and matters he did not want to hear about[50] -

and thus does not fall prey to the type of deconstruction that Derrida inflicts upon Fukuyama's end of history. Blanchot's short text is thus the perfect summary of the logic of hauntology as both a deconstruction of the empirical end of history and an essential rupture of ontology, and the importance of taking both the empirical and the essential themselves into account.

The recovery and reaffirmation of this metaphysical reading of Derrida, spectrality and hauntology is vital to the reconfiguration of the problems of the future at work here. It is precisely the affirmation of the importance of a rigorous metaphysics, of both temporality and ontology, which opens up the space of a possible escape from the apocalyptic present. Thus it is important to remember and reclaim the *essential* futural and ontological element of hauntology rather than using it as an critical reading strategy for the *empirical* stasis of the post modern condition after the ends of art and history.[51] Hauntology is not a nostalgia for lost times, past or future, or the malaise of the endless apocalyptic present of the end times. Rather it is the logic of the aporia made material in the disruption of the ontology of presence and, like *écart*, the activation of the dead time of the living present that opens up towards the space of the future.

Chapter 6

Small Library Apocalypse

The ideas of the *grammè*, *différance* trace and spacing are all part of the grammatological method used to deconstruct the logocentric underpinnings of all metaphysico-theological discourse. In doing so it is necessary that they hold a certain relationship to the metaphysics of time, as shown above, and also to the historical determinations of both history and the philosophy of history in every instance. Examining this relationship reveals another important manifestation of the inter-action between philosophy and the future in Derrida's work. The specific mention of the future as a problem of the future anterior has already been mentioned above, however this is indicative of wider implications for both history and the future within Derrida's work. Derrida's understanding of the logocentric nature of metaphysics and his deconstructive project mirror his methodological structure of the trace-*écart*, that is they give both an historical analysis (the past) and a way beyond the limits of such historification (the future). The historical situation with which Derrida is engaging is what he calls either the epoch of the logos, of onto-theology, or even the metaphysico-theological epoch. This is a philosophical determination of history in terms of metaphysics of presence, which Derrida takes from Heidegger's analysis of the history of philosophy. This in turn is based upon the historical progression found primarily in Hegel but also in particular in Nietzsche's construction of history as both the development and overcoming of nihilism.

Derrida's project is explicitly philosophical in two ways. Firstly, it is part of the tradition of philosophy described above. Secondly, it is explicitly engaged with the philosophical ideas of such traditions. The methodology he employs is structured around a close reading of the text; however this does not mean that his criticism is purely textual as many critics seem to assume. Rather, such close textual analysis reveals points of stress within the metaphysical concepts and/or assumptions. The most obvious of these is the contrast between the metaphysics of presence espoused by many of these texts and the way in which writing is considered within such metaphysics, and the compensatory concept of the book employed to counter-balance this discrepancy. It is this antimony that provides the main basis for Derrida's linguistic science of grammatology. However, grammatology itself is only a methodological tool for deconstructing metaphysical discourse and eventually the possibility of metaphysics itself, a project that must function from within the limits of metaphysics and hence must actively engage with such concepts. In fact such limits are an integral part of the Derridean project. It is often by looking at how the concept of metaphysical limits function and how such concepts may be pushed to their limits, that deconstruction progresses. The analysis of the logic of the aporia is a perfect example of this engagement with and re-thinking of the metaphysical limits of philosophy.

This is the clearest conception of Derrida's project as a whole: The investigation of the relationship between limits and the possible, or impossible and aporetic, progression beyond such limits. This structure has already been explored in three different ways above: Firstly, in terms of nuclear criticism as the way in which the nuclear epoch is connected to the epoch of literature; secondly, in terms of writing and in particular the epoch of the book. While it is these two manifestations of limits and progression that are particularly pertinent to the idea of experimental literature, it is the third set of limits that underlies both of these. This third limit is of course the epoch of metaphysics: the logocentric privileging of presence that has taken place throughout the entire history of philosophy. Hence, as a whole Derrida's philosophical project is about the conditions of possibility of philosophy, the limits implicit in such conditions, and finally, the possibility of progression beyond such limits. This is the philosophy of the future, both as an explicit examination of the future and of philosophy. The dual movement between limits and progression in Derrida's philosophy is all brought together by the idea of the *envoi*, or, destination. This is such a central theme in all of Derrida's thought that he not only gave the title "Coups d'envoi" [Sendoffs][1] to his schematic examination of how philosophy should be taught; but also organized the entire structure of philosophical education around the concept of destination. The centrality of this theme highlights the importance of Heidegger to Derrida's thought, in particular the Heideggerian concept of the path. In *Sendoffs* Derrida writes:

> It seems clear enough that the meditation on the history of being, after the existential analytic, opens the question of the [ontico-] ontological difference onto what it always seems to have "presupposed" - in a sense not purely logical - implicated, enveloped, namely *a thought of the sendoff*, of *destination*, and of the *gift*.... The same necessity appears, even if in another manner, *mutatis mutandis*, for what I have tried to demonstrate under the heading of *différance* as sendoff, differentiation, delay, relay, delegation, tele- and trans-ference, trace and writing in general, destination and undecidability, etc.[2]

The change in direction and opening up in philosophy that occurred after the existential analytic has already been discussed in Chapter 5, through the logic of the ghost and hauntology, which Derrida develops directly in response to the aporias of death appearing in Heidegger's existential analytic. Already hauntology has brought ontology into question, but the notion of the sendoff begins to work through the outcomes of this problematization and the potential futures of the history of being that it suggests.

This connection between the ontico-ontological difference and the resulting sending has also been explored as part of the discussion of Derrida's sixth missile/missive of nuclear criticism. Despite the fact that Derrida leaves his examination of the nuclear condition off this brief summary of his work, it is clear that the *envoi* is an important theme, especially in relation to the history of literature and philosophy and their respective futures; which means that this relatively minor text on nuclear criticism warrants the in depth examination given here. The important thing to note here is the way in which the text on nuclear criticism makes connections in opposite directions firstly to the concrete technological situation of the world and secondly to the work of literature (and also philosophy) under such conditions.

Likewise, Derrida uses the theme of destination as a way of organizing such problematics so that they are open to the explicitly philosophical critique that operates through the question of the ontico-ontological difference and the *envoi*. This means that destination may act as a mediator, or point of connection between the discourses of philosophy and the conditions of the world. Nuclear criticism is an excellent example of such mediation, but it is not the only one possible. Derrida gives a list of other such areas of inquiry:

destination and destiny, all the problems of the end and thus limits or of confines, ethical or political aim, teleology - natural or not -, the destination of life, of man, of history, the problem of eschatology (utopian, religious, revolutionary, etc.), that of the constitution and the structure of the sender/receiver system, and thus of the dispatch or sendoff and the message (in all its forms and in all its substances - linguistic or not, semiotic or not), emission, the mission, the missile, transmission in all its forms, telecommunications and all its techniques, economic distribution and all its conditions (producing, giving, receiving, exchanging), the dispensation of knowledge and what we now call the "orientation" ["*finalisation*"] of research or of techno-science, etc.[3]

There are many possible research topics here. The present work is included amongst them. The question of the relationship between the end of art and the end of history is a perfect example of the thought of the destination of these two discourses. The entire question of the philosophy of the future is much like the problem of eschatology, in that it seeks to give an underlying structure to the way in which utopian, religious and revolutionary thought are all possible, and the implications of such a structure of thought.

Included within Derrida's structure of destination are several interesting implications for the future of literature and art in general. Given the way in which literature is emphasized in the work on nuclear criticism, and the connections drawn between this and the discourse of the end of art, the structure of the *envoi* may give an important insight into the nature of experimental literature and the possibility of art in general (and its relationship to philosophy) within Derrida's work. In *Sendoffs* Derrida groups his discussion of art and aesthetics under the heading of 'Poietics'. This is a particularly Heideggerian move which will become apparent in the examination of Heidegger's conception of the work of art in Chapter 7. Derrida states that he uses the title of "poietics" because it: "has the merit of recalling a double dimension: theoretical and necessarily discursive research on the one hand, and experimental, "creative," and performative research on the other."[4] This recalls the distinction and duality of missile/missives six and seven, between critique as translatability and the creativity of experimental literature. The hinge that unites these two dimensions is the apocalypse.

Derrida makes an explicit reference to his "small library apocalypse"[5] in *The Post Card*. This is an important point. It is via a reading of *The Post Card* that the connections between Derrida's wider philosophical project, *envoi* and experimental literature are made clear. *The Post Card* is a curious book within Derrida's *oeuvre*. It is not an explicitly philosophical work. That is, it is not written in the conventional philosophical style. Its first section is presented as a set of letters, from whom, to who is not made clear. Derrida does not help when he writes in the preface that: "You might consider them, if you really wish to, as the remainders of a recently destroyed correspondence."[6] In the same preface Derrida explicitly states that he signs these letters in his proper name, but then immediately casts the authority of this signing into doubt in a footnote.[7] What remains of the text, which is itself a text of remains, is the set of letters, or, to use the French, *envoi*. Here is the rub. The text is a set of *envoi*, of sendings or dispatches. As Derrida says, they might be read "as the preface to a book that I have not yet written."[8] This is an explicitly futural sending; as such it is the best example of what Derrida might consider experimental literature to be.

If experimental literature is motivated by the sending of philosophy, then what better form for it to take than as a set of dispatches? The set of *envois* that make up *The Post Card* range in subject matter, they break down the distinction between fiction and testimony, and also between literature and philosophy. They switch from in depth examinations of Heidegger, Freud, Socrates and other philosophers and the banal reporting of the everyday life of the writer, who may or may not be a fiction. As with nuclear criticism, the hinge this text turns upon is the apocalypse. The small library apocalypse referred to above is that which the book is named after, the post card. Firstly, the letter itself is part of the tradition of apocalyptic literature. The template for the apocalyptic genre, the Book of Revelation, is a letter sent from Saint John to the seven churches of Asia. A fact referenced by Derrida in 'No Apocalypse, Not Now.' As such *The Post Card* involves musings upon the structures of the dispatch making up the postal service, along with the sender/receiver system of the message. This connection is alluded to in the letter of 5 September 1977, where it says:

> I think that these are, you understand, the last letters that we are writing to each other. We are writing the last letters, "retro" letters, love letters on a bellépoque poster, but also simply the last letters. We are taking the last *correspondence*. Soon there will be no more of them. Eschatology, apocalypse, and teleology of epistles themselves.[9]

In itself, this quote makes no clear connection between the *envoi* of the letters and eschatology and apocalypse. But this is the entire point of *The Post Card*. It is not a work of philosophy, rather the form of the text, as a set of *envoi*, mirrors the form of that branch of philosophy that is concerned with the apocalypse, eschatology. The uniting factor here is the destination that is at the heart of philosophy as understood by Derrida. Hence, it seems that *The Post Card* is an attempt to engage with philosophy by using that which is at the same time its innermost essence and yet is also excluded from the traditional domain of philosophical writing, the creativity of experimental literature. This is the *envoi* as both the ultimate revelation of philosophy, the destination of its essence, and at the same time its apocalypse, a way beyond that comes from the beyond, a retro-apocalyptics of the future perfect. This is an explicit comment on the possibility of philosophical discourse that makes up the second manifestation of the apocalypse in *The Post Card*, the apocalypse of philosophy. The "post card apocalypse"[10] of *The Post Card* refers to one found by its author in the Bodleian library, upon which the *envois* are/were written. This post card has an illustration taken from a medieval fortune-telling book (a book of prophecy, a writing of the future). It is apocalyptic because it reveals Socrates writing while Plato stands behind him and instructs; thus reversing the conventional history of philosophy: that Socrates spoke and Plato wrote. The reversal of the history of philosophy is also its destruction (its deconstruction). It also returns to the heart of Derrida's work, the problem of language. *Of Grammatology* starts by reinforcing the conventional view of the history of philosophy with a quote from Nietzsche: "Socrates, he who does not write."[11] This simple quote watches over the deconstructive project. It alludes to the Nietzschean attack on Platonism then taken up by Heidegger as an attack on metaphysics, and reinterpreted by Derrida as an attack on logocentrism. Hence, the post card (both book and card) reverses this history of philosophy and hence also disrupts the historical determinations of writing. If Socrates were to write what would he write? Surely it would not be the logocentric determinations of Plato/metaphysics? The radical possibility suggested by this echoes the call for the end of the book and the beginning of writing, which is the central claim of *Of Grammatology*. It is such disruption and reversal, such deconstruction, which motivates the sending of the apocalyptic *envois* in *The Post Card*. In this regard the form and structure of *The Post Card* as *envoi* is again important. In this case it is how such a structure moves away from the encyclopedic model of the book. *The Post Card* does not present itself as a work of philosophy in the sense that it moves in a logical progression from one subject matter to the next until the entire domain of its subject matter is encompassed and unified by its arguments and discussion. Instead the structure of the *envoi* works at all levels. Socrates sends dispatches to Freud and vice versa. Personal correspondences are invaded by these sendings of ideas, and such letters promote further sendings into the nothingness beyond the text. This could easily serve as a metaphor for Derrida's work as a whole: as a footnote in one text points towards another reading that disrupts the first text, or what is elliptical in one piece is elaborated in another. Reading Derrida then becomes a process of tracing out the paths of these sendings between each other and back to their senders and receivers, or between their different readers, who perhaps pass them on to the next destination.

Writing and literature are integral elements of all of Derrida's philosophy. His method of deconstruction is explicitly based around an analysis of the place of writing within the history of philosophy. This in turn operates within a wider set of philosophical determinations, namely the logocentric epoch of ontotheology or metaphysics. By developing grammatology, a rigorous philosophical method of expressing the way in which all the aporias of text function in relation to the various logocentric contexts of the text, Derrida proposes a movement beyond this metaphysico-theological epoch. Such movement takes the form of a sending or destination, which becomes a central theme within Derrida's work. Because Derrida's method functions by operating directly on texts it is also in this form that any changes arising (dispatched) out of his work will take. The conclusion developed here is that this new form of writing will be experimental literature. This necessarily encompasses the *envoi* as a poietic ideal and this concept of poiesis will be developed below with regard to Heidegger. *The Post Card* is an excellent example of how all these ideas function together. However, while it has many similarities with the idea of experimental literature suggested in 'No Apocalypse, Not Now,' there is a significant point that it does not seem to deal with. This is of course the idea of the connection between literature and the death machine.

This connection appears explicitly at the start of Japanese author Kenji Siratori's debut novel *Blood Electric*, which carries the warning that "THIS MACHINE KILLS."[12] Siratori's book also fits within the experimental model of literature Derrida has already connected with the nuclear epoch. The death it warns of could well be the death of literature at its own deconstructive hands. Referents float through the text detaching and attaching seemingly at random, there is no grammar to talk of, unless it uses a secret grammar of its own creation. The book is a literal example of the destinerrance of the nuclear sending; it literally has no end as the text wanders off the last page, to be continued in all Siratori's writing. In these ways Siratori fits perfectly with the death machine literature of the nuclear epoch. Interestingly enough he also fits perfectly with the futurist idea of literature. Marinetti, who was in particular highly influenced by Stéphane Mallarmé,[13] spoke explicitly of the connection between literature, dynamic movement and death. In the 'Founding Manifesto of Futurism' he writes: "Up to now literature has exalted a pensive immobility, ecstasy, and sleep. We intend to exalt aggressive action, a feverish insomnia, the racer's stride, the mortal leap, the punch and slap."[14] Futurist literature is already the death machine Derrida identifies with the production of literature. Marinetti goes further and spells out how this new futurist literature will differ from that of the past. This is done in his 'Technical Manifesto of Futurist Literature,'[15] which when compared to Siratori's book might even appear as an instruction manual. In particular this can be seen in Marinetti's calls for the destruction of syntax (the end of grammar) and the abolition of punctuation. In their stead he proposes a new set of symbols, the mathematical plus, minus, equals, etc. In Siratori's case it is the symbols of the Internet that make up this new punctuation, the colon, back slash and greater/less than signs of HTML. This connection of the literature of futurism and that of nuclear criticism as both the sending of the death machine is the final step in the synthesis of the two into a new discourse of nuclear futurism. In some senses this synthesis may merely be an illusion and it would be possible to say that futurism is none other than a monument of the nuclear epoch. This contention aside, what this synthesis, the new discourse it produces, allows is a confrontation with the problem of the secondary element of the (non) event of 1984, the end of art.

How is it possible to construct the artistic discourse of nuclear futurism out of this conjunction, if indeed such a thing is possible? The answer to this lies in Derrida's final statement of missive/missile six when he writes:

> Hence we meet once again the necessity and the impossibility of thinking the event, the coming or venue of a first time which would also be a last time. But the destinerrance of the sendings is precisely what both divides and repeats the first time and the last time alike.[16]

This quote could almost be a direct answer to the central problem of this book; the necessity and impossibility manifested as the (non) event of 1984. In many ways this answer has lain dormant throughout this book, the answer in question is contained within the idea of the event as a repetition of the hauntological temporality of the first time and the last time. Both event and invent which are two central pillars of nuclear futurism already contain within them the idea of a sending. They both derive from the Latin *venire*, to come, event via *evenire*, to come forth, and invent via *vertere* to turn. The connection to the French *envoi* is obvious. The event is the obverse of the sending of nuclear futurism. If the sending is an endless wandering that is the result of criticism, then the event is what appears, or to foreshadow the discussion of the event, what comes forth, in this sending. It is in this way that the event is what will allow an analysis of the end of art. This, of course, refers to the way in which Heidegger configures both sending and the event with regard to his critique of art in 'The Origin of the Work of Art'.

Chapter 7

The Work of Art and the Dangers of Technology

The event is an important idea within Heidegger's later philosophy, from the mid 30s onward. The German term he uses is *Ereignis*, which also refers to the idea of owning, property and proper (*eigen*) and is often translated as propriative event or just propriation. Heidegger uses the event to reformulate the problem of Being in a way that is beyond the ontico-ontological difference and outside or beyond the determinations and censures of Being.[1] Already it is evident how the event mirrors the escape from the ontico-ontological difference previously configured in terms of speed. In this sense *Ereignis* is an important element in Heidegger's critique of metaphysics. This critique proceeds by the way in which *Ereignis* operates in a dual manner. Ziarek describes this operation as such:

> *Ereignis* names then an occurring in which what comes to be is given into its own. But it is given into its own in a manner that also de-propriates, that is, in coming to be what it is, a being (*Seinde*) discloses the withdrawal of being (*Sein*) as the nonground (*abgrund*) of its being.[2]

This description highlights the way in which *Ereignis* functions within the ontico-ontological difference, that is the difference between beings (*Seinde*) and Being (*Sein*), in a particular way which takes account of this very difference and the relationship thereof. *Ereignis* draws out the way in which the appearance of beings is also a withdrawal of Being. By explicitly functioning within and recognizing this dual motion of appearance and withdrawal *Ereignis* reveals the abyssal nature of all beings, the absence at the core of all presence. This function of *Ereignis* has several important corollaries, which Ziarek identifies:

> *Ereignis* draws out relations and carries them in their abyssal, nongrounded occurrence. It thus draws relations into what is "proper" for them: the *Abgrund* of the scission of being and time. The emphasis in such experience falls upon the futural temporality of such de-cision and the absence of the ground which is "experienced" precisely as the movement of propriating. Thus, Heidegger's notion of *Ereignis* is an "instant" critique of subjectivist, empiricist, and essentialist ideas of experience. It ungrounds their assumptions, disclosing the propriating (*ereignend*) force of the dispropriating (*enteigend*) abyss (*Abgrund*) of being. To undergo such and experience ... is to experience the carrying out of the futural unfolding of being as an event ungrounded, "properly" drawn out and de-cisioned, in the dispropriating temporality of its giving.[3]

There are two elements here that are vital to nuclear futurism. The first is the way in which *Ereignis* itself provides a critique of various doctrines of philosophy - subjectivity, empiricism, essentialism and, although it in not explicitly mentioned, truth. The second is the emphasis on the futural nature of *Ereignis*; as an aside, despite the fact that the future is explicitly mentioned twice within this summary, this important futural element seems to then fade away from Ziarek's further application and investigation of *Ereignis* with regard to the avant-garde. The future is exactly what is at stake in the discourse of nuclear futurism. Hence, the Heideggerian conception of *Ereignis* fits perfectly within the structure already constructed by the Derridean discourse of nuclear criticism. It both is a way out of the bind of the ontico-ontological difference and a clear example of how this escape must be futural. However, these metaphysical aspects of *Ereignis* only show one side of how it fits within the ideas of nuclear futurism. The obverse side is made clear when the ways in which it appears within Heidegger's work are examined. In particular this will provide an analysis of art and language, along with a critique of truth, which together will both complete and ground the ideas of nuclear futurism.

Heidegger makes an explicit connection between *Ereignis* and art. In the addendum to 'The Origin of the Work of Art' he writes: "Art is considered neither an area of cultural achievement nor an appearance of spirit; it belongs to the *propriative event* [Ereignis] by way of which the "meaning of Being" (see *Being and Time*) can alone be defined."[4] The metaphysical implications of this in terms of the connection between *Ereignis* and the "meaning of being" have been described above. Hence, the next important step is to examine how it is that art can be considered as *Ereignis* and what are the implications of this with regard to the ideas of technology and the avant-garde.

Central to Heidegger's theory of art is the way in which he understands the art work in its work-being rather than its object-being. The work which is done by the art work is the way in which some particular beings come to stand in the light of their being.[5] The example Heidegger gives is the way in which a pair of boots painted by Van Gogh both opens up the world of a peasant woman and also hides this world behind the earthly equipment of the boots. What is revealed here is the relationship between the earthly equipment of the boots and the nature of equipmental being within the world; this relationship is the relation between beings and Being the ontico-ontological difference refers to. The work-being of the work of art is the unconcealment of this relationship. In Greek unconcealment is given the name of *aletheia*, which is then translated as truth. Hence this relationship is what the boots are in truth.[6] This understanding of art has two important implications. The first is that art is now no longer understood as mimetic, it is no longer about the representation of objects. Secondly, this analysis of art in terms of unconcealment provides the base for a wider critique of the correspondence theory of truth. Taken together these two implications are clearly connected to the critique of a mimetic understanding of the future as a future anterior, developed above as part of nuclear criticism. Hence, by developing these two implications it will be possible to flesh out these areas of nuclear futurism with specific attention to art, truth, and representation.

Understanding truth as unconcealment is not entirely divorced from truth as representation. As Heidegger points out representation is already dependent upon some form of unconcealment. The correctness of the representation relies upon its connection to that which is concealed. Indeed the very possibility of representation is built upon the processes of concealment and unconcealment.[7] It is this relationship between unconcealment and concealment at the heart of truth. Heidegger writes:

> The essence of truth, that is, of unconcealment, is dominated throughout by a denial. Yet this denial is not a defect or a fault, as though truth were an unalloyed unconcealment that has rid itself of everything concealed. If truth could accomplish this, it would no longer be itself. *This denial, in the form of a double concealment, belongs to the essence of truth as unconcealment.* Truth, in its essence is un-truth.[8]

The appearance of beings is their unconcealment, but each revelation also closes off other appearances, conceals other truths. This initial concealment also conceals itself; it hides its own concealedness behind that which is unconcealed. The complete revelation of the world is not possible; however, this is not, and never was, the nature of truth. This critique of truth is linked to several important points, which have been mentioned above. Firstly, the deeper understanding of truth as unconcealment instead of representation clearly ties in with the way in which nuclear criticism rejects the understanding of the future in terms of the representation of the future anterior. The double concealment of truth is exactly how the problem of future futurity functions, the future as the future anterior always conceals itself behind its own futurity; it conceals the truth of a now which is always-already futural, the future perfect. This then connects the future perfect of nuclear criticism with the way in which it is also an epochal suspension of absolute truth. Secondly, in many ways these ideas about truth tie in with what Danto identified as the end of art. Danto claimed that the end of art arose because it became apparent that there was no essential *truth* of art that would allow any particular art to define itself as true art. At first this seems similar to the claim that the essence of truth is un-truth. However, this is not in fact the case, rather than rejecting the possibility of any connection between truth and art Heidegger draws them intimately together. This works on two levels. Firstly, this relationship itself is rethought. Art can no longer be considered in terms of the truth of art as what is and what is not 'true art,' the very proposition of true art would itself conceal the truth of art as unconcealment. In this sense rather than looking for some sort of truth of art to which the artwork must conform, truth is already at work in any artwork. It is here that the second level of connection between art and truth becomes apparent. By thinking of truth in terms of uncon-cealment rather than correspondence Heidegger rejects the mimetic element of art. Art is considered in its work-being rather than its object-being. This means that art must be regarded by the way in which it sets truth to work, that is, how it discloses the world, rather than how it corresponds to the world. Because of this the distinction that Danto makes between works of art and mere real things becomes impossible. Again this seems identical to the claims that Danto made concerning the end of art. However, while Danto breaks down this distinction with the example of Warhol's *Brillo Box* he also maintains it at a theoretical level. The distinction is always operating in the sense that the lack of distinction, the absolute mimesis is still a correspondence and hence a representational element to the way in which the *Brillo Box* as art is considered. Of course the objectness of the artwork cannot be avoided even if it is not regarded mimetically, nor as the essence of the artwork. The artwork still exists as an object, and it exactly this existence that must now be considered.

The two levels discussed above with relation to Danto's theory of the end of art also reveal an important conjunction that must be taken into account. That is the connection between an understanding of art as truth and the actual artwork itself. This connection will reveal art, in both senses, as *Ereignis*. Throughout the above discussion of art and truth what has continually been presupposed is the artwork itself. How will the artwork fit within this theory of art when it has already been said that what is important is the work-being and not the object-being of the artwork. The artwork in its work-being has two sides. The first, discussed above, is the work done by the artwork as the work of truth. The second is the way in which the artwork is itself something that has been worked. Hence, its object-being is already dependent upon its work-being. The way in which these two sides are connected is made clear through the idea of *techne*. *Techne* is both the Greek term for art and/or craft, and at the same time also denotes a mode of knowing. This mode of knowing is a bringing-forth of beings out of concealment and as such is a form of unconcealment.[9] What is central to this way of thinking about the artwork is a fundamental understanding of it as something that has been created. Hence, it is in terms of this createdness that the artwork may be examined.

According to Heidegger createdness "reveals itself as strife being fixed in place in the figure by means of a rift."[10] This is a very dense and abstract statement; there are three important ideas at work here. The first is the idea of strife. It is through strife that the artwork opens up a world; this is the strife between the earth on which the artwork stands and the world which it opens. Strife is the way in which the *Ereignis* of art functions, the fundamental connection between the two sides of the ontico-ontological difference which occurs in the work of art in its work-being. The second important idea it that of the figure (*Gestalt*). This is the actual artwork, which is brought forth by *techne*. The figure is the way in which the work of truth is fixed in place in the artwork itself. Importantly Heidegger says that the "figure (*Gestalt*) is always to be thought in terms of the particular placing (*Stellen*) and enframing (*Ge-stell*) as which the *work* occurs when it sets itself up and sets itself forth."[11] The connection between the figure and what Heidegger calls enframing is particularly interesting as it points towards the relationship between art and technology, which he explores in 'The Question Concerning Technology.'[12] This relationship is pertinent to the discussion about the avant-garde and nuclear futurism and how they are linked to this relationship. The third and final element of the characterization of createdness is the rift and the way in which it both reveals createdness as strife and also holds it in place in the figure. This is most apparent in the equivocation of the German word for rift: *Riss*. This word means both rift in the sense of a crack or tear, and in this sense echoes the abyssal nature of *Ereignis*, and also inscription such as a rune, letter, design or drawing. This second sense is highlighted by the related verb *reissen*, which literally means writing. Hence, the rift is both the abyss of the strife and the inscription of the figure. Together this establishes the created work of art as *Ereignis*, as something that both works and is worked.

These three elements of the created work of art - strife, the figure and the rift - provide three ways in which it will be possible to draw out the implications of this conjunction of art, and nuclear futurism with reference to the problems of the avant-garde and the development of nuclear futurism. The important nexus of this conjunction, and that which has not been discussed in depth so far, is the idea of technology. Already a link between art and technology has emerged from the discussion of art. This link was anticipated by the use of *techne* and completed by the way in which the figure is thought in terms of enframing (*Ge-stell*). In his inquiry into the essence of technology in 'The Question Concerning Technology' Heidegger develops technology as a mode of bringing forth. This is already obvious from the etiology of the word 'technology' which has its roots in the Greek *techne*. The way in which technology discloses the world is as standing-reserve. This means that the world is seen merely as resource; the forest as lumber, the river as hydro-electricity, the mountain as ore-deposit. This revealing goes so far as to include man himself within this mode of disclosure, until there is no other possible mode of disclosure. It is at this point that Heidegger says: "We now name the challenging claim that gathers man with a view to ordering the self-revealing as standing reserve: *Ge-stell* (enframing)."[13] Here is the point of connection between the work of art as a figure and the essence of technology; they both function by the *techne* of enframing. Initially this seems like an unusual claim because the work of art is not immediately so intimately entwined with technology. What this does reveal is Heidegger's next important point: that the essence of technology as enframing is not itself anything technological in the sense that machines are technological.[14] Enframing is a way of revealing the world that orders and challenges it. As such, technology is a mode of *aletheia* and a functioning of truth; however, this relationship between truth and technology has itself become problematic. While enframing reveals the world as standing reserve it also conceals its own unconcealment. It reveals the world as present and itself as the truth of that world, never the truth as the unconcealment of the world. This is the way in which the representational theory of truth is able to develop and operate - by concealing its own unconcealment. This leads to a secondary concern for Heidegger. In this way enframing detaches man from the truth. Technology only allows man to encounter himself via the technological mode of thought, as something present to which the truth must correspond. Man is detached from the essence of truth as unconcealment, he is only revealed in his technological being, as an object and never in his abyssal nature as something unconcealed. Technological man of enframing can only encounter himself in the world, that is himself as a technological being and the world as the world of absolute knowledge through enframing. In this sense man is also detached from his essence as a knowing subject that reveals truth as unconcealment. Enframing drives out all other modes of revealing and establishes itself as the truth of the world, but as a truth that does not reveal its own truthful essence.[15]

Heidegger sees this essence of technology in enframing as something dangerous. He writes:

> What is dangerous is not technology. Technology is not demonic; but its essence is mysterious. ... The threat to man does not come in the first instance from the potentially lethal machines and apparatus of technology. The actual threat has already afflicted man in his essence. The rule of enframing threatens man with the possibility that it could be denied to him to enter into a more original revealing and hence to experience the call of a more primal truth.[16]

There is an important distinction here between the actual machines of technology and what may be called the technological mode of thought. The danger lies in the latter rather than the former. In this way it may be possible to redeem the fascination the futurists had for the machines of technology while still allowing them to participate in a critique of the modes of thought which surrounded them. Already this way of thinking about technology has allowed a rethinking of the connections between technology and art evident in various avant-garde discourses. It is no surprise then that this is exactly the direction in which Heidegger moves in his discussion of this danger of the technological mode of thought. At this point Heidegger quotes from Hölderlin's *Patmos*, again recalling the connection between apocalypse and the missive, and says: "But where danger is, grows / The saving power also."[17] As the danger of technology develops more and more, as enframing hides its own nature as unconcealment, this growth also signals a saving which is a return to the essence of the technological as a mode of unconcealment. The saving power grows because the technological mode of thought as enframing provokes a new questioning of its own essence. Precisely because enframing hides its own essence as unconcealment the question of essence becomes pertinent as something absent. In turn this questioning returns to the essence of technology as unconcealment.[18] Heidegger writes: "The granting that sends one way or another into revealing is as such the saving power. For the saving power lets man see and enter into the highest dignity of his essence."[19] Here, in the form of the saving power is the sending or the *envoi*, which is central to Derrida's nuclear criticism. Just as the *envoi* sends a way out from the danger of the apocalyptic wandering of the nuclear referent the saving power returns to the essence of truth as unconcealment. The sending of the saving power also returns to the nature of art as *techne*; and it is as art that Heidegger envisions the saving power. He writes:

> Because the essence of technology is nothing technological, essential reflection upon technology and decisive confrontation with it must happen in a realm that is, on the one hand, akin to the essence of technology and, on the other, fundamentally different to it.
> Such a realm is art.[20]

Both technology and art are modes of unconcealment or *techne*, and because of this they are intimately connected. However, while the *techne* of technology functions only by enframing, art also reveals the way in which the figure of such enframing is also revealed as strife and is held in place both over and by the rift. The intimate connection between art and technology as modes of unconcealment means that as the danger of technology grows the saving power of art also emerges. While the technological mode of thought denies its own truth as unconcealment art always reveals the strife of its own revelation. This draws man back into the domain of truth as unconcealment.

This kinship between technology and art provides a framework within which is it possible to examine both the problems of the avant-garde and the development of nuclear futurism. The avant-garde, and in particular the futurists, show the moment of the danger of technology and the redemption of art perfectly. By drawing the technological into the realm of art they subvert and save *techne* and return it to its own essence. This is evident in the way in which they take up the machines of technology and flirt with the most dangerous apparatuses. The danger lies not in these machines themselves but in the mode of thought used to produce them. The work of the avant-garde is to thrust these machines back into the rift and in this manner reveal their own *techne*. Of course the most dangerous machines of modern times are without doubt nuclear weaponry. Hence, it is logical that at this most dangerous moment the avant-garde must or should be at its strongest. Nuclear weapons illustrate perfectly the conjunction between technology and art. The aporia of the nuclear referent is the point of turning, the sending of the saving power. It shows how the technology of nuclear weapons holds truth in epochal suspension; that truth must operate as the continual unconcealment of destinerrance. This is the motor of the production of art, or, as Derrida puts it, literature. This drawing together of the danger of nuclear weapons and the way in which art becomes vital, gives new strength to the thrust of the avant-garde in the form of nuclear futurism.

Chapter 8

Only a Remembrance

So far the conjunction between art and technology has been considered by using the artistic mode of revealing as primary. However, this approach precludes several important factors. These are the way in which technology reveals art and the consequences this has on artistic production and the domain of the avant-garde. The technological mode of thought - enframing - also subsumes the work of art. The result of this is the institution-alization of art by the art industry. Heidegger writes: "[T]he works themselves stand and hang in collections and exhibitions. Yet are they here in themselves as the works they themselves are, or are they not rather here as objects of the art industry?"[1] Here, as they hang in museums, the artworks are no longer encountered in the way that they reveal the world. The work-being of the artwork has perished and all that remains is the object-being of the enframing of the artwork as standing-reserve. But how does this happen? Heidegger writes:

> As soon as the thrust into the awesome is parried and captured by the sphere of familiarity and connoisseurship, the art business has begun. Even a painstaking transmission of works to posterity, all scientific efforts to regain them, no longer reach the work's own being, but only a remembrance of it.[2]

The art industry is the enframing of the artwork. It is where invention gives way to inventory. As art becomes an institution - the museum, the gallery, an investment option - the works of art themselves become institutionalized, imprisoned within the apparatus of the art industry. They no longer open up the worlds they once did, they are now merely objects of aesthetic appreciation, historical incidence or monetary value. They no longer participate in the unconcealment of the world. They are concealed from the world just as it is from them. The most obvious example of this enframing of art is the museum. By removing artworks from the world in which they are produced, and as a result are also producing, the museum quarantines them; it is the very apparatus of their enframment. Since their development in the late eighteenth and early nineteenth centuries the museum has come under constant criticism as the mechanism of the death of both art and history. This is most apparent in the affinity between the words museum and mausoleum, which connects the museum with all sorts of cultures of necrology and death.[3] Quite literally the museum is the death of art because it removes it from life and the lived world. As soon as the artwork is removed from the world out of which it was created it is no longer has any meaning other than a purely aesthetic appeal. It is removed from its context and left to die. For example, the statue in a Greek temple is not merely a representation of the god; it opens up the devotional world of the temple. When the same statue is removed from the temple and placed in a museum, possibly even in a different country, the power of the statue to open up the world within the temple is lost. The museum has killed off the devotional structures and cultures, which once provided the context within which the statue was put to work. Likewise, the museum does not participate in the process of history; it merely provides an image of it and in this way creates a history no longer connected to the present of the museum. Both the art and history of the museum are disconnected from the praxis of life; they are no longer immanent to the culture that created them. Instead they are held in suspension by the prophylactic of the museum solely as objects of detached contemplation. Hence, all that is possible is an aesthetic criticism of the artwork as an object of beauty. A similar attack has been leveled at modern critical philosophy. Criticism favors contemplation, judgment and analysis to such an extent that it precludes any action or active involvement with the world.[4] It cannot influence any action; only investigate it in a detached manner.

The homogenization of art as aesthetics by the museum was exactly the target of avant-garde artists.[5] The futurists in particular held the museum in contempt for exactly the reasons outlined above. Marinetti, with his usual vitriol and hyperbole, outlines this attack in the 'Founding Manifesto of Futurism':

> Museums: cemeteries!... Identical, surely, in the sinister promiscuity of so many bodies unknown to one another. Museums: public dormitories where one lies forever beside hated or unknown beings. Museums: absurd abattoirs of painters and sculptors ferociously slaughtering each other with color-blows and line-blows, the length of the fought-over walls.[6]

This is part of the futurists overall attack on the past. The museum is not only a symbol of all the artistic conventions they wished to break free from. It is part of the mechanism that reduced these conventions to purely aesthetic conventions in the first place. The museum is not only the cemetery, the monument to the corpses of past art, it is also the abattoir which killed them in the first place by reducing them to aesthetic objects and making their monumentalization possible. More sinister still is the effects which the museum has on the artists who visit them. They supervise and structure all artistic thought and all modes of artistic production. The aesthetic mode of thought seeps out of the museum and begins to contaminate artistic production itself. Art becomes an atrophied limb of the art industry.[7] As a result Marinetti gives an explicit dictum to artists to attack and destroy the museum:

So let them come, the gay incendiaries with charred fingers! Here they are! Here they are!... Come on! set fire to the library shelves! Turn aside the canals to flood the museums!... Oh, the joy of seeing the glorious old canvases bobbing adrift on those waters, discolored and shredded!... Take up your pickaxes, your axes and hammers and wreck, wreck the venerable cities, pitilessly!⁸

As an explicit physical attack against museums this dictum gave a concrete manifestation to the futurist's desire to break free of history. However, this attack exposes an aporia at the heart of the avant-garde. By explicitly attacking both history and the museum the avant-garde inextricably ties itself to both of them. The museum becomes the context giving meaning to the art. For example, Duchamp's ready-mades only have their artistic meaning within the museum or gallery. Anywhere else the *Fountain* is merely a urinal, insofar as it is engaged with "life," while in the museum it is art.⁹ The art of the avant-garde only holds its revolutionary values so long as there is a history for it to escape.

The aporia may also, and indeed, must be approached from the other side. Showing how the avant-garde is intimately entwined with the museum also reveals the inverse, how the museum is also avant-garde. By killing history the museum is also engaged in the work of the avant-garde. If works within the museum are removed from their historical context then the museum empties out lived history by removing all of its content. The museum is effectively engaged in the avant-garde project of the destruction of history. This returns to the revolutionary origin of the museum. The Louvre Museum was established in 1793 with exactly this purpose in mind. It was to bracket off the pre-revolutionary history of France. To level the historical playing field, so to speak, and provide a *tabula rasa* in order to allow the new age of the revolution to come-forth in its own right

detached from the France of the past. By aesthetically neutral-
izing the art of the past the museum shows how such art has no
place or significance in the new revolutionary age.[10] New art for
the new age must be produced, the conditions which define the
context of the world have shifted, there would be no place for the
art of the past within this new context anyway. Already both
history and its art are meaningless and hence the contextlessness
of the museum is the only possible context for this art. By
'preserving' - petrifying - art and history the museum also
destroys it, this mirrors the way in which in attempting to
explicitly escape and destroy history the avant-garde also must
continually reference it. Both are bound within this dialectic
which, when considered from both sides, forms the production of
both history and art and their death.

This dialectic, or aporia, is a perfect example of the necessary
connection between art and technology. It is not possible to
simply say that technology is opposed to art or vice versa that art
is simply critical of technology. Rather, they must be viewed in
this dialectical relationship as they two different expressions of
poiesis. Indeed the museum could be seen as technology at its
most dangerous. When the technological mode of thought
engulfs art itself, rendering it to pure aesthetics and/or monetary
value, this is best described by the name reification. Yet this must
always give forth the saving power, the avant-garde seeks to
regain art from the danger of the museum, to give it new vigor
while at the same time repeating the museum's destruction of all
prior art. The danger of the institutionalization and aestheticization of art by the museum is exemplified by Danto's declaration of the end of art. The end of art occurred with a moment of
absolute mimesis - the Warhol *Brillo Box* - which made art
completely subservient to the museum. The *Brillo Box* as a
worked work of art, as opposed to Duchamp's ready-mades
which still provided a critique on work and making, reduced the
'truth' of the art to the object within the museum. The *Brillo Box*

is a perfect example of how the aestheticization of the museum reduces the truth of all art to truth as correspondence, or, mimesis. The museum effectively reinforces the concept of truth as correspondence and as a result is engaged in the concealing moment of enframement, which is part of the technological mode of thought. The aesthetic barrier of the museum is the concealment of the truth of art as unconcealment. Likewise, the museum also detaches itself from history; this is the other side of the end of art. By confining history to the museum it means that the production of art in the present is detached from this history. It is and can only be, to use Danto's phrase, post-historical art. Even when it is placed in the museum the artwork is detached from the rest of history within the museum by the museum's own mechanism of the destruction of context within itself. If the end of art identified by Danto in 1984 is really the epitome of the growing technological danger of the reification of the artwork by the museum and art industry, then there must also be a corresponding growth of saving power. How will the avant-garde respond to this increased danger?

All of this is pointing towards the avant-garde manifestation of nuclear criticism as nuclear futurism. Throughout history, in whatever form, nothing has presented more of an immediate technological danger than nuclear weapons. They are the ultimate danger and as such are also the source of the saving power of art. As a synthesis of the logic of the most dangerous technology and the impulse of the avant-garde nuclear futurism emerges at the point at which technology and art meet, the growth of the saving power. Nuclear futurism is explicitly engaged with the issues of history and the museum because of the way in which it is connected with the archive. The aporia of the nuclear referent repeats the dialectics of the museum and the avant-garde. It also functions by both being dependent upon and also the destruction of a very specific mode of history. The stock-piling of written texts in the archive is what makes literature possible, and it is as literature that the discourse of nuclear criticism is possible. It is only possible to conceive of the archive as such because of the possibility of its total and remainderless destruction by nuclear weapons. However, this conception is only possible as literature, the very thing that would be destroyed. The result of this aporia is on one hand the continual production of experimental literature, which is also a deconstructive movement; and on the other, an epochal suspension of history and truth. Nuclear futurism is defined by the very possibility of the destruction of the archive; this also entails an absolute deconstruction of history by the epochal suspension produced by the aporia of the nuclear referent. There is a clear similarity between the way in which nuclear futurism engages with literature and the archive and the way in which art and technology relates to the avant-garde and the museum. The avant-garde called for the destruction of the museum in order to free art from history, yet this also bound it tightly to both history and the technological forces of the museum. Inversely, the museum - structured around the preservation of history - also destroys it with a revolutionary impulse. Nuclear futurism repeats this motion by the way in which it is dialectically made possible by the archive and yet embraces the destruction of this very possibility via the deconstructive force of literature and the future perfect. The targets of nuclear futurism are also set upon the absolute truth of technology. Rather than the absolute revelation or unconcealment of truth that technology promises, by animating the aporia of the nuclear referent nuclear futurism inhabits the domain of truth as *aletheia* - the double movement of concealment and unconcealment, which is the work of art.

This fits within two important junctures. Firstly, the way in which the danger of the technology of nuclear weapons clearly is the origin of the saving power of art. This leads to the second point, the entanglement of technology and art at this origin, and the distinction between the technological mode of thought and the machines of technology. Nuclear weapons are undoubtedly technological machines - they use electricity, jet engines, computers, satellite tracking, etc. - and yet they do not function within the logic of technology - enframing. In fact, the logic they motivate, the aporia of the nuclear referent, itself destroys the technological mode of thought. Hence, the art of nuclear futurism, which must be obsessed with technology in the form of nuclear weapons and devices of all sorts, can do so without being consumed by the enframing of technology. As art nuclear futurism also belongs to and has its roots in the technology of nuclear weapons along with the technological mode of thought which ties it to the archive of history. The historical antinomies of the museum mirror the aporia of the nuclear referent and also locate this aporia at the point of the conjunction of the most dangerous moment of technology and the saving power of art. By putting the aporia of the nuclear referent to work within this conjuncture is to connect it back to the impulse of the avant-garde and to formulate the new avant-garde of the most dangerous technology as nuclear futurism.

Chapter 9

Language, Literature, and the Death Machine

Although nuclear futurism clearly fits within the schema of technology and art, as well as the museum, history and the avant-garde, and also provides a solution to the problem of the (non) event of 1984 with a new mode of futural thought, neither of these fully explain the nature of the actual work of nuclear futurist art and exactly how it is possible for it to do these things. In many ways this explanation has already been pre-figured. The development of nuclear futurism developed out of an examination of the aporia of the nuclear referent as developed by Derrida. Indeed, it is as a productive expression of the dialectic nature of this aporia that the art of nuclear futurism functions. The artwork is already governed by the logic of the aporia, already evident in the previous examination of the aporia as discussed in detail above. This art is, of course, literature. Literature is central to the aporia of the nuclear referent because it is the mode in which the aporia operates. However, this is only one side of the story. Literature also puts the aporia to work in its experimental form which returns to the power of the death machine. As an experimental death machine literature embraces its own deconstructive power, the aporia which governs it, and which only becomes apparent under the sphere of influence of nuclear weapons and the imminent risk of total remainderless destruction they hold. Experimental literature that appropriates its own death is the product of the putting the aporia of the nuclear referent to work.

Literature also returns to the point at which the explicit discussion of art and technology began above. This point is the sending of, and from, the aporia of the nuclear referent in the form of *Ereignis*. *Ereignis* has already been discussed above in the ways in which it functions in relation to art, but another account of *Ereignis* - in 'The Way to Language' - has important consequences for nuclear futurism in the way that it relates to language and how literature is located within this logic. There is already an important distinction evident here. Heidegger's discussion of language steers well away from literature. Instead he clearly says that language "is tongue, and works by word of mouth."[1] Such a definition takes language away from literature that is always written, and as defined above, is also dependent on the preservation of many writings in the archive. The relationship between literature and language has already been problematized, but this problem may turn out to be important in itself. The key to this problem, the distinction between language as showing (saying) and language as sign (writing), lies, for Heidegger, in a transformation in the essence of truth. It is the former configuration of language which Heidegger is interested in. He writes: "Saying [*Sagen*] means to show [*Zeigen*], to let something appear, let it be seen and heard."[2] Connections to truth as unconcealment are evident even her with the reference to letting things appear. The full evidence of language as *Ereignis* comes later when Heidegger writes

> *What bestirs in the showing of saying is owning.* .... Let us call the owning that conducts things in this way - the owning that bestirs the saying, the owning that points in any saying's showing - the propriating.[3]

Language as the showing of saying functions by propriating, as a propriative event, that is, as *Ereignis*. Propriating functions by opening a space of clearing for the entering of what is present, while at the same time allowing what is withdrawn to depart and also retain that withdrawal. This is the dual unconcealment of truth as *aletheia*, as discussed above in relation to art. There is then a clear point of comparison between art and language via the idea of *Ereignis*. Both art and language function as *Ereignis*, the propriative event which beings come forth and reveal their own groundedness in the abyss of being. This seems similar to how literature functions under the logic of the aporia of the nuclear referent. It is the revealing of its own conditions of possibility, which are also its conditions of impossibility. However, this comparison is not as straightforward as it first appears. Language as *Ereignis* is explicitly language as saying and not as writing, while literature is explicitly written word, which is possible because of the archive. The division goes further still, Heidegger has already pointed out a transformation in the essence of truth between these two forms of language. If they are to be brought together as the *Ereignis* of nuclear futurism then this division must firstly somehow be explained and secondly shown how it is dissolved by nuclear futurism.

A shift in the essence of truth of this sort has already been discussed above. This is of course the difference between the correspondence theory of truth and truth as unconcealment. The latter theory, truth as unconcealment, utilizes *Ereignis* and is evident is both the artwork and language as saying. Of more interest is the former, the correspondence theory of truth, this is the theory at the essence of writing, it is thus by examining how this theory functions that the connection between literature and art will become clear. Understanding truth as correspondence is only possible by a double concealment, firstly the concealment which is necessary in order for truth to come forth; and secondly a concealment of the first necessary concealment. This secondary concealment hides the absence that is necessary in all presence. This double concealment is given the name enframing, and it the way in which the technological mode of thought operates. There is a close kinship between the ways in which these two theories of truth operate with regard to *Ereignis*. Heidegger recognizes and explains this when he writes:

A thinking that thinks back to *propriation* can just barely surmise it, and yet can already experience it in the essence of modern technology, an essence given the still odd sounding name *Ge-Stell* [enframing]. The enframing, because it sets upon human beings - that is, challenges them - to order everything that comes to presence into a technical inventory, unfolds essentially after the manner of propriation, inasmuch as all ordering sees itself committed to calculate thinking and so speaks the language of enframing. Speech is challenged to correspond to the ubiquitous orderability of what is present.[4]

There are three important elements in this quote that need to be unpacked: Firstly, the close relationship between propriation and enframing. This occurs as a self-referential move. When unconcealment seeks to unconceal itself, it can only do so by falling into the technological mode of thought - enframing. This is because in ignoring what must remain concealed in unconcealment the double concealment of enframing begins. Secondly, the way in which enframing strives for a technical inventory. The idea of the inventory is exactly how the museum functions. The result of this is that the museum is severed from the world; it is a detached object of contemplation. It is also this logic that commands the archive, which makes literature possible. Thirdly and finally, because of the detachment produced by reducing language to an inventory the idea of truth as correspondence arises. Truth as an inventory of what is present is separated from the world and all that is possible is a correspondence between the two. When these three points are put together they give an account of how the essential shift in truth manifests itself as a shift in language from saying to writing. From poetry to literature and from the oral tradition to that of the printing press: Literature is the technologization of language.

Understanding literature in this way, as the technological form of language, fits perfectly with Derrida's claim that literature was contemporaneous with the nuclear epoch. They are both expressions of the technological domination of the world. However, it has also been said that as the art of nuclear futurism literature is also the saving power that emerges at the most dangerous moment of this domination. The art of nuclear futurism emerges at the moment when the technological danger is the greatest, as such, it can only emerge from the technological itself. If literature and the associated archive are the way in which language is dominated by enframing then they are the only possible form in which the saving power can emerge. The way in which the saving power is related to language is an important point that Heidegger picks up on:

> In order to think back to the essence of language, in order to reiterate what is its own, we need a transformation we can neither compel nor concoct. The transformation does not result from the fabrication of neologisms and novel phrases. The transformation touches on our relation to language. That relation is determined in accordance with the sending that determines whether and in what way we are embraced in propriation by the essence of language, which is the original pronouncement of propriation.[5]

There are two significant points in this quote that situate the manifestation of the saving power with regard to nuclear futurism. Firstly, Heidegger explicitly describes what the saving power is not. It is not the mere creation of new words and idioms. This relates to Derrida's seventh missile/missive, which drew out the consequences of nuclear criticism for criticism in general. This leads to the story of Babel and an understanding of criticism as nothing more than translatability, which abandoned criticism in a maze of endless wandering without end. In a radical form this translatability would result in the never-ending creation of neologisms and rephrasing which is exactly what Heidegger says the saving power is not. Secondly, in giving a positive description of the saving power Heidegger uses the idea of sending, which appeared in the form of *envoi* in Derrida's sixth missile/missive. He also shows how it is that this sending is related to *Ereignis*. In the discourse of nuclear criticism this connection was only tentatively spelled out, here is appears in full. The saving power of language is a sending of *Ereignis*. Nuclear futurism appears at the point when the technological language of literature begins to eat itself. The way in which this must manifest in literature is as an experimental deconstructive literature that embraces its own destruction, and along with it the destruction of the technological mode of thought. That will reveal its own conditions of impossibility. Conditions which must be technological and which take the form of the death machines of nuclear weapons, the absolute technological danger, the possibility of remainderless destruction.

Chapter 10

Death on a Pale Horse

An example of this experimental literature has already been given in the form of Kenji Siratori's *Blood Electric*, but one that reveals more about the concrete connections to art is Jake Chapman's *Meatphysics*.[1] As with Siratori's book, *Meatphysics* is a constant flow of sense and nonsense. Snatches of scientific history and psychophysics of biology are combined with a schizophrenic reasoning and the motifs of science fact and fiction. All of this looks as if it has been passed through the technological death machine of a corrupted computer file. The unused symbols of various fonts appear, repeat and disappear and so create a new grammar that grows to dominate the text. There is a creative transparency and the means of technological production are evident throughout the text. File names and system hierarchies create and punctuate whole passages, as if the entire text is the result of a machine cannibalizing itself as it continuously runs corrupted program procedures. The author has been concealed by the technological mode which created the book, the entire process of writing along with editing, saving, encryption as a binary language (perhaps an auto-critique), infections of computer viruses, hard-disc crashes and printing errors are all out in the open, enframed by the technological means of production. As with Siratori's book this demented logic can have no end. There is no progression throughout the text, made evident by the absence of that universal indicator of narrative vector, the page number. The final 'sentence' reads: "*a holocaust of words has no end*"[2] and is left open, lacking a full stop to indicate an end or completion of any sort. This is a literary holocaust, the total death of literature, which reflects the potential holocaust of total nuclear destruction. As with the epochal logic of nuclear futurism, this literary text is held in suspension without end. *Meatphysics* is a perfect example of the technological program of enframing, which firstly seeks to bring everything to presence and leave nothing unconcealed; and secondly understands all that is present as understandable and hence seeks to document it all. It demonstrates the way in which these two aims must cause a breakdown in the very system that sought to produce them. In bringing everything to light, the entire process of the production of the text as an object of literature, *Meatphysics* deconstructs any literary possibilities it may have held. It destroys its own narrative. This happens in two ways. Firstly, it must attempt to create a new grammar that can control the total translatability of its technological production. This can only result in agrammatical nonsense, any sense of time or progression is impossible under this logic. Secondly, the book can never end, and without an end from which is may be conceived of in its entirety it can never be an object; it is continuously a work of presencing. There is no numerical progression from one page to the next, each one conceals its obverse and creates a radically new event.

Chapman's book is of significance because it also provides a link to his work in other artistic mediums with his brother Dinos. As the blurb on the back reads *Meatphysics* is "[a] comparative journal for the Chapman Brothers' aesthetic work."[3] Although they have long since descended into self-parody (if indeed they were actually ever anything else) this link provides a path via which it is possible to explore how nuclear futurism may influence or even manifest in other artistic mediums beside literature. To confine the art of nuclear futurism to literature alone would be ridiculous claim. It would curtail art so viciously that it may fatally wound it, although in some ways this is the point. Hence, literature must still provide an important element in these other works in the form of the manifesto. Jake (1966) and Dinos (1962) Chapman have been producing art since 1993 when they produced the manifesto-like 'We Are Artists'. Their first big break came with the *Disasters of War* series, which consisted of making miniature models based on Goya's etchings of his experiences of the atrocities of the Peninsular War of 1808-1814.[4] The original Goya etchings are a perfect example of the process of the enframing of art by the museum. They were produced as journalistic documents of what Goya saw during the war. They are products of living through the atrocities he experienced. This original horror of the reality of what is depicted in the pictures has since been covered over by their acceptance into the art world as pure aesthetic objects. The Chapmans' appropriation and remaking in many ways reverses this process. By applying the low craft-like techniques of model making to reinterpret high art they are breaking the aesthetic aura and detaching the original Goya prints from their gritty and horrific origins. Working from within the context of the art industry the Chapmans' are able to subvert their own context and evaporate the processes of museification.[5] The horror of the Chapmans' miniatures is twofold, the original horror of the mutilated soldiers and civilians has been replaced by what in many ways is much more horrific to the art industry, the mutilation of art itself. This mutilation was taken a step further when, using the proceeds from their own artistic endeavors, the brothers purchased an original set of Goya etchings and vandalized them by replacing the features of a tortured soldier with a crude cartoon heads, or scratching a swastika tracing out lines of composition directly onto the original.

Horror is a big theme for the Chapmans. Their other work has included the 1996 exhibition 'Chapmanworld'. This consisted of a series of mutant children joined together into multi-limbed creatures with all sorts of sexual organs sprouting from their flesh in various places. Given names like *Zygotic Acceleration, Biogenetic De-sublimated Libidinal Model (Enlarged X 100)* these creatures could well be the result genetic modification gone wrong or the mutants spawned as a result of radioactive contam-

ination after a nuclear exchange; both a result of the technological terror of the current age and/or the near future. More
recently 'Artifacts From the Family Chapman' has moved in the
other temporal direction. It appears to be a collection of tribal
masks and artifacts not unlike those that inspired Picasso at the
birth of modern art in the early twentieth century.[6] The significant difference here is that the Chapmans' artifacts are all
branded with the ubiquitous golden arches of the MacDonald's
corporation. They are not the anthropological artifacts that they
first appear but are in fact totems of the corporate world. Perhaps
their most significant work to date is the now destroyed *Hell*
(1999-2000). A giant diorama in the shape of a swastika is
populated by over 5000 model Nazis, mutant experiments,
corpses, scientists and skeletons, all involved in various atrocities; there is no clear logic or narrative, Nazi soldiers load each
other into ovens, the bodies are half naked and often have
mutilated genitals and limbs, mutants with multiple appendages
experiment on hapless soldiers in bizarre laboratories, or just
consume random body parts; there is a puppet show involving
human corpses with wires running through their hands, feet and
heads which lead up to gruesome puppeteers above them; there
are machines made of body parts mixed with machinery; in one
place the dead are brought back to life by some sort of reani-
mation plant; there are mass graves and at the center of the
swastika where the four arms meet, is a volcano out of which the
whole maelstrom erupts. Violence begets more violence for its
own sake in what the Chapmans have described as a sort of
eternal return that plays on a constant loop.[7]

Hell was part of an exhibition held at the Royal Academy of
Art in London in the year 2000 called *Apocalypse: Beauty and
horror in contemporary art.*[8] Holding this exhibition in the
millennial year perhaps tempted fate, but it is also not the first
time that the apocalypse has made an appearance at the Royal
Academy. In 1775 a drawing by John Hamilton Mortimer was

exhibited there entitled *Death on a Pale Horse*. This is in reference to Revelation 6:7 where upon the opening of the fourth seal on the book of life John writes: "And behold a pale horse; and his name that sat on him was Death, and Hell followed with him."[9] As such the drawing depicts the events occurring at the end of the world according to Revelation, the events of the apocalypse itself. Mortimer's drawing is important because it is often considered the first in an artistic tradition known as the apocalyptic sublime.[10] The idea of the nuclear sublime has already been considered and rejected as a representative theory of art above. This then begs the question, what use is this return to the sublime to nuclear futurism. However, like mimetic art in general, along with the idea of the future anterior, nuclear futurism may allow a rethinking of the idea of the sublime, and indeed, this even may be necessary to the idea of nuclear futurism. The apocalypse has already been encountered in the course of this paper in two ways: Firstly, as the threat of total nuclear war; and, secondly, in the apocalyptic destinerrance of criticism under the logic of the aporia of the nuclear referent. It is fitting then that the development of nuclear futurism will return to the idea of both the apocalypse and the apocalyptic.

In a similar fashion it is fitting that the discussion of art and the problem of the end of art should also return to the juxtaposition of beauty and horror, which in many ways is the central issue of much of modern art. One of the main contentions of modern art is an exploration of the place and function horror and ugliness may take within art. This question is not new; the art world has already grappled with it in various forms. It originates in Edmund Burke's 1756 text *Philosophical Enquiry into the Origin of Our Ideas of the Sublime and the Beautiful* where he describes the main characteristic of the sublime under the heading of 'Terror'. He writes:

No passion so effectually robs the mind of all its powers of acting and reasoning as fear; for fear being an apprehension of pain or death, it operates in a manner that resembles actual pain. Whatever is terrible, therefore with regard to sight, is sublime, too.[11]

There are two important points here. The first is that by operating in a manner which resembles actual pain, and that in being an apprehension of death, the sublime in art operates in much the same way as the death machine of literature. The sublime is not just a representation of that which is terrible it operates by the very production of the fear of death. This is precisely the second point. The sublime is not merely representation. This is what is developed in Kant's discussion of the sublime in *The Critique of Judgment*. For Kant the sublime is that moment when representation breaks down and is no longer possible.[12] Taken together these points clearly show how the sublime, in this form, ties in with the ideas of nuclear futurism. It destroys representation and is a machine of death. This must lead to a rethinking of the way in which art functions which has in some ways already been attempted by the avant-garde, and in particular the futurists. Interestingly it also leads back to the Heideggerian idea of *Ereignis*.

All of these points are drawn together in an essay be Jean-François Lyotard called 'The Sublime and the Avant-Garde.' As with the above, Lyotard formulates the sublime not as a sort of representation but as something that happens now. This is not as simple as it seems because the understanding of such a happening must always precede itself with the question 'is it happening'. The now of the happening is that which is opened up by the questioning of the happening itself. Lyotard understands this as an event, or, he points out, as what Heidegger called *Ereignis*.[13] Heidegger's conception of art in its work-being rather than its object-being is closely ties up with this question of happening. In 'The Origin of the Work of Art' he writes: "What is art? We seek its essence in the actual work. The actuality of the work has been defined by that which is at work in the work, by the happening of truth."[14] Like the abyss at the root of Heidegger's conception of *Ereignis*, Lyotard's happening is held in possibility by nothingness. This nothingness is the constant threat of nothing happening. The happening now of the question 'is it happening?' is held as a question by the possibility that nothing might happen. Art as sublime, as something that happens now, is always created in the face of the possibility of not creating art, the possibility of nothing happening.[15] The discourse of the sublime holds two different explanations for the anxiety which gives rise to this possibility. Kant explained it as the transcendental function of the sublime as the moment at which the faculties of the senses are overwhelmed by the event of an absolutely large object or the absolutely powerful. These absolutes can only be comprehended as objects of reason and hence are beyond all possible expression. This produces a dislocation of the faculties, which perhaps is not unlike Rimbaud's aim to produce a disorder of the senses,[16] which in turn produces the anxiety in the face of potential nothingness and hence the questioning of the happening, the sublime.[17] The second explanation is Burke's. Here the anxiety and the questioning of the happening is a result of the terror arising in the face of death, the absolute nothingness.[18] Taking a more Heideggerian line will perhaps combine these two explanations to some extent by developing the essential finitude of transcendental philosophy in terms of death. Regardless, the outcome of either of these explanations is the same. Nothingness must always be held at bay by the happening that occurs as a result the very questioning provoked by the anxiety and/or terror felt in the face of nothingness. This happening is the production of artwork. Art shocks people and by this shock gives evidence that something is happening.

Such art, shocking art, is precisely what the avant-garde

aimed to produce.[19] Yet there is also a more fundamental conclusion to be drawn from this discourse on the sublime. If the sublime is the happening that happens in the face of nothingness then it also returns to the question Heidegger defined as the fundamental question of metaphysics 'why is there something and not nothing?' This question has now been answered; there is something as a result of artistic production, as a sublime happening. Art is the production of the world. There is also an important temporal element to this answer. The happening must always be the production of something new, something going beyond all prior events and pushes the boundary of what has happened. This continual pushing into the domain of the nothing and the production of events is none other than the progression of history. Heidegger also saw art as a driving force of history, he writes: "Whenever art happens - that is whenever there is a beginning - a thrust enters history; history either begins or starts over again."[20] It is this movement' of history forward into the future and which makes history itself possible. In this sense art contains the paradoxical nature of history within itself. In order to move forward history must break with itself but this break can only come from the historical conditions of the present, these conditions are only made evident once the new perspective of the progression of history reveals them as history.[21] It is art that allows this synthesis of the now and the new; but just as this synthesis provides a critique of the possibility of history, it also provides one of temporality itself.

If art as the sublime is the motor of history then this must also produce its own critique of temporality, and in particular futurity, which will connect up with those given above with regard to nuclear criticism and hauntology. The sublime happening of the *Ereignis* can be in no other time than the now. However, this happening is also the continual production of the new. The only way in which these two, the now and the new, can be reconciled is by the temporality of the future perfect. This is made clear when in his analysis of the work of art Heidegger writes: "The establishing of truth in the work [of art] is the bringing forth of a being such as never was before and will never come to be again."[22] This temporality is futural in the sense that it never was before - it is the new. But this futurity is also perfect; because it will never come to be again it is not a mere representation of something that will come again in the future - a future anterior -it is happening now. The temporal logic at work here is that which Derrida proposed for both the aporetic advent of the event of nuclear war and the temporal disruption of hauntology: the happening for the first and the last time. Art as the sublime thus connects up with the temporality of the future perfect of nuclear criticism and provides a temporal grounding for the art of nuclear futurism. This also is a very strong argument against Danto's theory of the end of art. Art must always operate in the domain of the future; it simply cannot be disconnected from this historical progression, such a statement is absurd. There can be no such thing as post-historical art because art itself is the force of history. It always motivates the temporality of the future perfect, which drags art into a future that is now. It is the happening of history and the history of happening; or, to use Derrida's terms the opening of *écart* and the trace that produces it.

Lyotard's discussion on the sublime also reveals another important point of connection between the sublime, the theory of nuclear criticism and the art of nuclear futurism, which not only provides a secondary line of attack against Danto, but also connects art back to questions about language, and in particular rhetoric, criticism and the manifesto. Part of Lyotard's discussion of the sublime concerns an analysis of an ancient treatise on the subject attributed to Longinus. This treatise is interesting because of the connections it draws between the sublime and rhetoric. How is it possible to talk of the sublime, and is the sublime possible in rhetoric? The sublime is problematic for the discipline of rhetoric because it is often associated with silence.[23] This is something Heidegger touches upon in 'The Way to Language' when he writes: "A human being may be speechless with astonishment or terror. He is altogether astonished, thunderstruck. He no longer speaks: he is silent."[24] There is an antipathy between the sublime and language, and yet also a co-dependence. Later Heidegger says: "Silence corresponds to the noiseless ringing of stillness, the stillness of the saying that propriates and shows."[25] There is reciprocation between silence and saying which resides at the core of *Ereignis*. This relationship is vital to understanding the sublime and how it relates to nuclear futurism. Between the two poles of the silence of the sublime and language is the happening of the event as the art of nuclear futurism. This indicates a possibility of a relationship between the sublime and rhetoric. Lyotard articulates the answer that Longinus suggests as the proposition that "inversions of reputedly natural and rational syntax [are] examples of sublime effect."[26] This is the domain of experimental literature such as that of Marinetti, Joyce, Beckett, Siratori and Chapman. However, it must be remembered that this experimental literature, which embraces the destructive force of the aporia of the nuclear referent and utilizes the power of literature as a death machine, appears as a very specific point in the discourse of nuclear criticism between the two conclusions of missiles/missives six and seven. The first of these conclusions - missile/missive seven - was the apocalyptic wandering of criticism as total translatability. This is the problem that lies at the center of the possibility of language, the problem of Babel. Still, in its apocalyptic nature this wandering still contains the possibility of the destruction of language itself, or Blanchot's second slope of literature. This destruction takes the form of the sending of the event hinted at in missile/missive six: the second conclusion Derrida draws. As a destruction of the nucleus of criticism this is the event that halts language and stuns it into silence. However, this event is also the sublime happening and as such is apparent as a work of art. Experimental literature is the mediator between these two, the art of nuclear futurism as both the babble of criticism and the silence of the sublime. It is both the origin in the form of the aporia of the nuclear referent and the end as the sending of the aporia. It is the alpha and the omega that unites genesis and apocalypse in the temporality of the future perfect - 'at the beginning there will have been' – for the first time and the last time.

Chapter 11

For the First Time and the Last Time

Nuclear futurism contains an important connection between art and literature. This connection has been most evident throughout the history of art in the form of the manifesto. By considering the manifesto in light of the understanding of experimental literature as both the origin and end of art as a sublime happening it is possible to reconfigure the position of the manifesto in relation to the art work. Rather than considering the manifesto as a philosophical transformation of the same ideas with which the art work is engaging, in the way which Danto does; or simply considering the manifesto as a statement of intent which informs or prescribes the form and/or content of the artwork; it is now necessary to consider the manifesto as in some sense both of these, the origin and the end which unify the work of art. The manifesto is vital to avant-garde art as nuclear futurism because it is what opens the futural space within which the artwork will manifest. This opening is the destruction of history and the epochal suspension of the future perfect. Literature is the force of the future because of the functioning of the aporia of the nuclear referent. The manifesto also serves a secondary function of the historification of the artwork. Once the artwork has set history in motion it then becomes part of that history which it has created. In some sense this rewrites history in the terms of this work of art and it is the job of the manifesto to articulate this process of historification. The work of art rewrites the history of art by locating itself in the future. Historification is an important element of the avant-garde, but this must be understood in the sense that it is the work of art that makes history possible and not vice versa. The historicity of the artwork arises as a critical translation of the artwork from the future perfect of its happening into different modes of discourse that recontextualise it in the progression of history which it has created. These two sides, the event and the criticism, must function together; and it is this point that is brought out in the artistic logic of nuclear futurism. The aesthetic interpretation of art is replaced by a speculative one whereby the dual movement of the work is synthesized by the event and its criticism into a force of the future. A future which is the fabulous perfection of the work of art held in epochal suspension by the aporia of the nuclear referent.

Conceptions of history, historification and historicity such as those developed above return to the questions of the end of history and the end of art with which this book commenced. These questions are also now revealed in their full Hegelian nature due to the development of the two concepts of the absolute and the sublime. The Hegelian notion of the end of art, and the basic logic of this notion is repeated as the end of history as well, is that: "For us art no longer counts as the highest mode in which truth fashions an existence for itself."[1] Art has been surpassed by philosophy as the premier mode in which the truth is manifest. This is exactly the point upon which Danto bases his theory of the end of art. For him art has exhausted all possible explorations of truth it possibly can. The evidence of this is the absolute mimesis of Warhol's *Brillo Box*. However, considered through the lens of the theory of art which has been constructed as nuclear futurism what this return to representation theories of truth shows is not a transformation in truth which surpasses art but rather a concealing of the unconcealedness of truth which is part of the technological mode of thought; a transformation that suppresses rather than surpasses the essence of truth. The difference between these two modes of historical thought and the way in which art is considered as part of this historical progression can be seen in the way in which the two concepts of the absolute and the sublime are used in each of these discourses.

Nuclear futurism rethinks the absolute in terms of the suspension of absolute truth; the epoch of absolute knowledge is not a complete revelation of the truth, but rather the *épochè* of absolute knowledge. The result of this suspension is that the sublime is not something that can go beyond this epoch but rather it must be questioned within this epoch - 'is it happening?' The future perfect will always be beyond in one sense, it is fabulous; but in another in its questioning and its criticism, its literature, it will give rise to the *Ereignis* of art, the work of historical movement within the suspension of the nuclear epoch. Fredric Jameson characterizes the end of art declared in the sixties as "the end of the Sublime, the dissolution of art's vocation to reach the Absolute."[2] In a sense this is what happened in the sixties, the art industry came into its own as the commodification of the artwork. Pop art is a particularly good example of this as it took the objects of commodities as the objects of art, but everything was still an object and it could do no work. The technological mode of thought was dominant here; art was an aesthetic object and its only relationship to truth was one of mimesis. Under the logic of the commodification of the beautiful as an aesthetic art object and truth as representation, which are both in connected in a Platonic way, art becomes no more than a spectacle; and as a spectacle the artwork also reveals its spectral nature. At the same time it is reduced to mere image, and also is subjected to the forces, powers and discourses of the market and criticism, which determine the meaning of this image without any need to reference or be held in relation to the actual reality of the art object. Just as the logic of commodity fetishism reduced the table to the dancing and sensuous non-sensuous of exchange value through the abandonment of the reality of the object, its actual use value and the phenomenological good sense that maintained this object, so too does the commodification of the artwork reduce art to its own image as representation, and its perception away from unconcealment and towards pure aesthetics without object.

As with the end of art the temporal logic of nuclear futurism provides an answer to questions concerning the end of history. Such answers have already been developed with respect to the problem of the (non) event of 1984, however the implication these answers have for art and philosophy still require further discussion. The future perfect of nuclear futurism, held in absolute epochal suspension by the aporia of the nuclear referent, is a vital rethinking of the image of the future and the influence, and indeed direct connection, of the future for art and philosophy. The future perfect is intimately connected with the Heideggerian conception of *Ereignis* and in particular via the way in which Lyotard develops this event as a questioning of the happening. The future perfect of nuclear futurism is a temporality as the happening of the future. Importantly what this means is that there is a direct engagement with the events of the future. In contrast, utopian temporalities disconnect from any happening, and indeed must be disconnected in order to be represented in the 'present'; the future perfect is the very happening of the future now. In this sense there must be the sort of epochal suspension Derrida talks of because there is no possibility of moving beyond the future-already-happening. This solves the fundamental problem of future futurity that characterizes all utopian thought. Rather than waiting for the future to come, which engages exactly the logic of disconnection, the future perfect is the questioning of the happening of the future. This direct connection between happenings and the temporality of the future perfect is exactly the sort of invigoration of the future that nuclear futurism aims for. What this logic means is that the future is the happening of events, the future is already happening now. This reclaims the future for the present as futural events. The to-come of the future is not a mere possibility but is the possibility of all happening. The future is happening and it is by these happenings that the future is coming, each time for the first time and the last time.

It is exactly this sort of temporal logic Derrida means by the strange concept of the messianic without content, evoked in *Specters of Marx* in connection with the conditions of possibility and impossibility of the *arrivant* and the return of the *revenant* [ghost] in its place. He elaborates on this concept with his retelling of Blanchot's *Writing of Disaster* where upon the appearance of the Messiah on the outskirts of Rome he is recognized and asked 'when will you come?' It is the questioning of the coming of the Messiah that is important in the conception of messianic time. The actual arrival of the messiah would undermine the to-come of messianic logic, it would be the end of the future and as such destroy both time and history.[3] It would be a disaster; and this disaster is precisely what is glorified by the idea of the end of history. It proclaims the actual arrival of that which will end history, be it absolute freedom in Hegel's case, or the triumph of liberal democracy in Fukuyama's case. Either way the proclamation of such an arrival would undermine the structures of thought that allowed the possibility of a progression towards such an end in the first place. Of course, what this close connection between messianic time and disaster points towards is the way in which the messianic must also be apocalyptic. The arrival of the Messiah would be a disaster, and a disaster of this magnitude would be none other than the apocalypse. Messianic time is characterized by the impossibility of the possibility of the arrival, or as Derrida puts it *arrivant*, of the Messiah, which is always reworked into the ghostly return of the *revenant* in his place. This aporia is made most apparent in its nuclear formulation as the aporia of the nuclear referent. What the discourse of nuclear futurism develops is the connection of this temporal logic of hauntology and the future prefect with the experiential structure of *Ereignis* as happening, which gives a clear conception of the future perfect as the happening of the future. Considering this happening as the possibility of the

113

questioning of the happening points to a specific relationship to the domain of criticism. It is here that there is a confrontation with the idea of the end of history and an answer to how such an 'end' is different to the suspension of nuclear futurism. Answering such a question will also show how nuclear futurism is able to confront itself in both its messianic and, in many ways more urgently, its apocalyptic natures. History still occurs under the logic of nuclear futurism; however history must also be rethought as a form of criticism rather than a temporal category. In order to draw this distinction out the place of criticism within the logic of nuclear futurism must be considered.

Derrida identified two outcomes of the aporia of the nuclear referent. The first was the sending of the event outlined in missive/missile six, and which lead to the examination of the Heideggerian idea of *Ereignis* and all that entailed. The second outcome was for the domain of criticism and the problems which nuclear criticism held for it. Nuclear criticism strikes at the very nucleus of criticism. It explodes the possibilities of criticism and reveals it as absolute translatability. As such all that criticism is capable of is the representation of the past. It is exactly as the repetition of this representation that history is recorded. Historical narratives are not events but the symbolic representations of various happenings. In this way history is a monumentalization of these events, a symbolic repetition distancing itself from the actual happening. History must be considered as a narrative rather than an actual temporal event. There are no temporal events other than those happening now, the happening of the future. By explaining the relationship between the two conclusions of missive/missiles six and seven nuclear futurism develops an analysis of the place and power of history in relationship to both the happening of the future and the way in which this is connected to the work of art.

The concept that ties these two conclusions together is that of the sending (*envoi*) as destinerrance. It is the endless wandering of criticism, and it is nuclear criticism that reveals this, which bursts apart the nucleus of criticism itself and sends forth the sending of the event. The dual consequences of this sending are the epochal suspension in the nuclear epoch and the temporality of the future perfect, which goes hand in hand with this suspension. Together this futural suspension is both messianic and apocalyptic, but at the same time is also historical. History, that is history as symbolic repetition and absolute translatability, always must function as destinerrance, and as such is linked to the sending of the event. It is the questioning of the event that does not cause the event but which always a futural element of the event: The 'when will you come?' questioning of the messianic. In this way the future appears as part of historical development, but this appearance properly functions via its inverse. History can only appear in the space of the epochal suspension of the future perfect, but it cannot move beyond its own wandering; the translation is never absolute, the revelation is never complete. This is why destinerrance is always an apocalypse without apocalypse; it is the errance of destination.[4] Both the critical translatability of history and the suspension of the future perfect function via this logic of apocalypse without apocalypse, which is always and can only be apocalyptic. However, it is now possible to think the apocalyptic in a positive sense. Of course the positive sense of the apocalyptic is precisely the messianic. However this positive thought goes further and it is expressly as apocalyptic that this positive conception will hold its power. This power is the ability of the apocalyptic to confront the possible and actual horrors of the world - the four horsemen of the apocalypse war, famine, pestilence and death - as well as Jameson's logic of capitalism imagined as the end of the world.

The positive manifestation of the apocalyptic functioning under the temporal logic of the future perfect may be clearly understood via the conception of the apotropocalyptic. This word combines the danger of the apocalyptic with the apotropaic, a means of defense that assimilates a small part of the danger in order to defend itself against the whole.[5] Rather than the apocalyptic horrors of war, famine, pestilence and death being mere harbingers of an apocalypse which is always to-come they are in fact elements of the apocalypse itself. This fits perfectly with the temporal logic of the future perfect and the existential structure of *Ereignis*. Instead of the apocalypse being a utopian, or rather, dystopian future futurity it is in fact always already happening now. The happening of the now includes the futural elements of the apocalyptic within its own event. What this means is that the such horrors are no longer disconnected from the present by the always to-come of the apocalypse, there can be a direct interaction with them as the apocalypse is a happening which is happening now rather than a possible, and yet also impossible future. The horrors of the future are happening now. Because of this nuclear futurism is able to directly interact with these horrors, can confront and deal with them. It is the task of nuclear futurism to occur as the happening of these horrors and hence it has a power over them that various utopian modes of thought do not. This also reveals an important conceptual shift which affects the way in which the critique of historical horrors functions. Just as the future perfect of apotropocalyptics negates the distance between now and the horrors of the apocalypse it also reveals the distance of the symbolic repetition of the horrors of history. In the face of the happening of the apotropocalyptic the symbolic repetition of the horrors of the past are revealed as detached and pale. However, the logic of total remainderless destruction governing nuclear futurism cuts deeper into historical criticism. Total destruction destroys the possibility of any such repetition or criticism. This itself seems horrific, and yet it is also that which brings criticism to life. It compels the sending of the event that is nuclear futurism, which is a direct confrontation with the happening of the apocalypse. In the light of nuclear futurism, shining from and into the future perfect criticism and critical theory are today cast into relief as the monuments and mausoleums of modernity, technology, literature, art, and ultimately, history.

Conclusion

The emergence of the future perfect as the first time and the last time, developed through the maneuvers of nuclear futurism, explodes the terminal stasis of the time of ends and the apocalyptic present of the end times. It does this not by providing a new vision of the future, still merely to come, but by revising the new itself as a futural now, an event that opens up the future in its very happening. There are two important sides to this re-envisioning of the future as the futural. The first is that this can only take place from within the context of the end times; that the new futurity must be formed from the very negation of the future in its present failure and the fragmentation of finality. This is the critical side of the argument, but it is a criticism that remains trapped within its own limits, always condemned to the endless wandering of destinerrance. Secondly, from within the stasis of this endless wandering and the aporias it generates, there is sent the *envoi* of the possibility of the event as an opening of the future.

By incorporating the poison of the end within itself criticism can burst apart its own limits and open itself up to this sending into the future in such a way that the dangers and horrors of those very ends can be confronted and overcome. The apocalypse is no longer either put off into the future, never present, or only appearing as a proliferation of apocalyptic horrors in the present; it can now be subject to critique and constant confrontation. The aporias of the ends of art and history are perfect examples of this dual movement. As the limits of each are subjected to critique through the discourses of futurism, nuclear criticism and hauntology they begin to ossify, historify and ultimately fragment under the futural force they reveal in their very happening. The end of history and the triumph of capitalism, imagined as the end of the world as in Jameson's image, is now put to work by this aporetic and apocalyptic logic, incorporating the danger of the apocalypse into itself and through this critical repetition sending forth a futural way out of the dead-end of history.

The operation of the two moments of destinerrance and the *envoi* have been examined and explored through writing and experimental literature as the death machine of language. This evocation of literature as death machine returns to Blanchot's conception of the two slopes of literature and begins to sketch out the matters at stake here. Blanchot's two slopes reflect the destinerrance of criticism and the sending of the event in terms of the death of reality at the hands of language and the return to matter through the death of language. Following the Derridian and Heideggerian implications and interpretations of the dual deaths of literature emphasized the temporal elements of the structure of the first time and the last time of hauntology and the event of the future perfect.

Temporality, however, is only ever half of the story. If the sending of the event is the *how* of the question 'is it happening?' then the *what* of the happening still remains opaque. The opacity of these remains returns to the spectral materialism developed through reading Blanchot's two slopes of literature against Derrida's concept of the specter. To read the happening of the event as the drag of matter back through, and from, writing, literature and critical philosophy, perhaps opens up the spectral future as a speculative project, one that is still happening and remains to come.

These then are the fragments of the present from which a new world can be built. However this new world is nothing other than the one that is already present, but which cannot be seen because we are always looking towards an impossible future. Only through the suspension of the future and the return to matter through the explosion of the kernel of criticism and its ends and limits, for the first time and the last time, can this world condense around us. The temporality of the future perfect is the first step in this speculative project, but the spectral nature of this step is the next that must be taken.

Footnotes

Introduction: Terminal Documents

1   These ends are found respectively in: T. Adorno, 'Cultural Criticism and Society', in, T. W. Adorno, S. Weber & S. Weber (trans.), *Prisms.* (London: Neville Spearman, 1967); G. Agamben, V. Binetti & C. Casarino (trans.), *Means Without End: Notes on politics.* (Mineapolis: University of Minesota Press, 2000); A. C. Danto, *After The End Of Art: Contemporary art and the pale of history.* (Princeton: Princeton University Press, 1997); J.-F. Lyotard, 'The Postmodern Condition: A report on knowledge', in, W. McNeill & K. S. Feldman (eds.), *Continental Philosophy: An anthology.* (Oxford: Blackwell, 1998); and, F. Fukuyama, 'The End Of History', in, *The National Interest.* Summer 1989.

2   F. Jameson, 'Future City', in, *New Left Review.* 21, May June 2003. p. 76.

3   The best analysis of the triumphs of capitalism still remains Guy Debord's analysis of the integrated spectacle as the union of the diffuse spectacle of capitalism and the concentrated spectacle of communism, found in *Comments on the Society of the Spectacle.* M. Imrie (trans.), (London: Verso, 1990), which originally appeared in 1988, a year before the fall of the Berlin Wall. It is no surprise then that Giorgio Agamben describes Debord as "the clearest and most severe analysis of the miseries and slavery of a society that by now has extended its dominion over the whole planet - that is to say, the society of the spectacle in which we live." in 'Marginal Notes on *Commentaries on the Society of the Spectacle.*' in G. Agamben *Means Without End*. The comment also provides the starting point of his argument for the end of television.

4   J. Derrida, C. Porter & P. Lewis (trans.) 'No Apocalypse, Not

Now (Full Speed Ahead, Seven Missiles, Seven Missives), in, *Diacritics.* 14(2) Nuclear Criticism, Summer 1984.

Chapter 1: The (Non) Event of 1984
1   K. Ruthven, *Nuclear Criticism.* (Carlton: Melbourne University Press, 1993). pp. 13-14.
2   M. Light, *100 Suns: 1945-1962.* (London: Jonathan Cape, 2003).
3   K. Ruthven, *Nuclear Criticism.* p. 15.
4   F. Fukuyama, 'The End Of History.' p. 3.
5   F. Fukuyama, 'The End Of History'. p. 18.
6   A. C. Danto, *After The End Of Art.* p. 22.
7   A. C. Danto, *After The End Of Art.* p. 27.
8   This wildly inclusive condition of art presents a problem for the traditional art critic: if anything can be art, including the everyday objects of the world, then art theory must also encompass and provide a theory for everything including all objects. Such a general theory of objects is metaphysics, which extends well beyond the scope of any art criticism. This represents a tension within art criticism, that it desires to use the metaphysical theories of philosophy and yet at the same time only wants to talk about art, which it can do only be maintaining some self-imposed and arbitrary limitation.
9   A. C. Danto, *After The End Of Art.* p. 13.
10 K. Ziarek, *The Historicity of Experience: Modernity, the avant-garde and the event.* (Evanston: Northwestern University Press, 2001). p. 4. See also 'Part Four: Crisis in the avant-garde', in T. Docherty (ed.), *Postmodernism: A reader.* (New York: Harvester Wheatsheaf, 1993). pp. 215-262.
11 K. Ziarek, *The Historicity of Experience.*

Chapter 2: The New Beauty of Speed
1   C. Tisdall & A. Bozzolla, *Futurism.* (London: Thames and Hudson, 1977). p. 9.

2   R. Hughes, *The Shock Of The New: Art and the century of change,* Updated and enlarged edition. (London: Thames & Hudson, 1991). p. 43.

3   R. Hughes, *The Shock Of The New.* p. 43.

4   R. W. Flint (ed.), *Marinetti: Selected Writings.* (New York: Farrar, Straus and Giroux, 1972). p. 42.

5   R. W. Flint (ed.), *Marinetti.* p. 41.

6   R. W. Flint (ed.), *Marinetti.* p. 41.

7   A metaphor for the ontico-ontological difference can be found in David Cronenberg's film adaptation of J.G. Ballard's novel *Crash.* Here the character Vaughan says to the eponymous main character Ballard: "That's the future Ballard, and you're already a part of it, you're beginning to see that for the first time there's a benevolent psychopathology that beckons towards us. For example the car crash is a fertilizing rather than a destructive event. ....To experience that, to live that, that is, that's my project." At which Ballard asks "What about the reshaping of the human body by modern technology? I thought that was your project." (for Ballard, via the car crash), here Vaughan replies, with obvious self-reference and parody from Cronenberg, "That's just a crude sci-fi concept, it floats on the surface and doesn't threaten anybody. I use it to test the resilience of my potential partners in psychopathology." It is then possible to see the crude sci-fi concept of technology as the ontic level and the deeper, beckoning psychopathology as the ontological, which underpins technology without being trapped by its crude and inoffensive lack of depth. This will become all the more apparent in Chapter Seven, through Heidegger's analysis of the structure and dangers of technology and its place within the ontico-ontological difference.

8   J. Derrida, 'No Apocalypse, Not Now.' p. 20.

9   J. Derrida, 'No Apocalypse, Not Now.' p. 20.

10   J. Derrida, 'No Apocalypse, Not Now.' p. 20.
11   K. Ruthven, *Nuclear Criticism*. p. 82.
12   R. Klein, 'The Future of Nuclear Criticism', in, *Yale French Studies*. 97, 2000. p. 79.
13   R. Klein, 'The Future of Nuclear Criticism'. p. 84.

Chapter 3: The Fabulously Textual Nuclear War
1   A wider examination of the nature of the aporia in general the centrality of this concept within Derrida's work will take place in Chapter 5
2   J. Derrida, 'No Apocalypse, Not Now.' p. 23.
3   J. Derrida, 'No Apocalypse, Not Now.' p. 23.
4   J. Derrida, 'No Apocalypse, Not Now.' p. 24.
5   J. Derrida, 'No Apocalypse, Not Now.' p. 23.
6   J. Derrida, 'No Apocalypse, Not Now.' p. 23-24.
7   J. Derrida, 'No Apocalypse, Not Now.' p. 24.
8   J. Derrida, 'No Apocalypse, Not Now.' p. 24.
9   J. Derrida, 'No Apocalypse, Not Now.' p. 26.
10   J. Derrida, 'No Apocalypse, Not Now.' p. 26.
11   J. Derrida, 'No Apocalypse, Not Now.' p. 26.
12   J. Derrida, 'No Apocalypse, Not Now.' p. 26.
13   J. Derrida, P. Kamuf (trans.), *Specters of Marx: The state of debt, the work of mourning and the new international.* (New York: Routledge Classics, 2006).
14   J. Derrida, 'No Apocalypse, Not Now.' p. 27.
15   K. Ruthven, *Nuclear Criticism*. p. 3.
16   J. Derrida, 'No Apocalypse, Not Now.' p. 27.
17   J. Derrida, 'No Apocalypse, Not Now.' p. 27.
18   J. Derrida, 'No Apocalypse, Not Now.' p. 28.
19   J. Derrida, 'No Apocalypse, Not Now.' p. 28.
20   The death of the individual and the temporal disjunctions produced by philosophy in attempting to deal with this death are expanded upon in Chapter 5 through the logic of specter that appears in Derrida's later works.

21 J. Derrida, 'No Apocalypse, Not Now.' p. 28.

22 J. Derrida, 'No Apocalypse, Not Now.' p. 28

23 For an explanation of the ideas of the trace and *différance* see Chapter 4 and the in depth examination and introduction to Derrida's philosophy therein.

24 J. Derrida, 'No Apocalypse, Not Now.' p. 28.

25 J. Derrida, 'No Apocalypse, Not Now.' p. 28.

26 J. Derrida, 'No Apocalypse, Not Now.' p. 30.

27 J. Derrida, 'No Apocalypse, Not Now.' p. 30.

28 See: J. Derrida, 'On a Newly Arisen Apocalyptic Tone in Philosophy,' in I. Kant & P. Fenves (ed.), *Raising the Tone of Philosophy: Late essays by Immanuel Kant, transformative critique by Jacques Derrida.* (John Hopkins University Press: Baltimore, 1998). This theme will reappear in Chapter 5 and its discussion of hauntology and the end of history.

29 The apocalyptic tradition of literature is started by the Book of Revelation which was a missive which St John sent to the seven churches of Asia Minor. This is an important point because it ties together several themes. Firstly the connection between the apocalyptic tradition and the sending/dispatch/missive/*envoi* this is the point which Derrida is picking up on and which will develop into the concept of experimental literature as subversive and revolutionary, and also plays out in 'No Apocalypse, Not Now' explicitly because of the way in which it is structured as a set of missives. Secondly, the connection between apocalypticism and revolutionary/subversive impulses ties in with all sorts of ideas about the new and the future etc. Together these points foreshadow firstly the importance of experimental literature and the place of the *envoi*, and secondly, the apocalyptic nature of all of this, which in some ways has been obvious, but this explicitly ties it to an apocalyptic tradition beyond the idea of total nuclear destruction as some sort of secular apocalypse, such as Marxism, socialism,

or in some ways, fascism.

30 J. Derrida, 'No Apocalypse, Not Now.' p. 30.
31 J. Derrida, 'No Apocalypse, Not Now.' p. 29.
32 M. Heidegger, D. F. Krell (ed.), *Basic Writings* Revised and expanded edition. (San Francisco: Harper Collins Publishers, 1993).
33 J. Derrida, 'No Apocalypse, Not Now.' p. 29.

Chapter 4: The End of the Book and the Beginning of Writing
1   J. Derrida, G. C. Spivak (trans.), *Of Grammatology: Corrected edition*. (John Hopkins University Press: Baltimore, 1997). p. 11.
2   J. Derrida, *Of Grammatology*. p. 12.
3   J. Derrida, *Of Grammatology*. p. 18.
4   J. Derrida, *Of Grammatology*. p. 18
5   J. Derrida, *Of Grammatology*. p. 4.
6   J. Derrida, A. Blass (trans.), *Writing and Difference*. (London: Routledge, 1978). p. xi. This is further complicated by Derrida's examination of Aristotle's use of *gramme* (line, trace) in *'Ousia and Gramme*: Note on a note from *Being and Time'*, in, J. Derrida, A. Blass (trans.), *Margins of Philosophy*. (Chicago: University of Chicago Press, 1982). See p. 34. n. 9. Of course the discussion of the concept of time in this piece is also of interest with regards to both Derrida's analysis of Heidegger and the futural elements within the work of both.
7   J. Derrida, *Of Grammatology*. pp. 84-86.
8   J. Derrida, *Of Grammatology*. p. 62.
9   J. Derrida, A. Blass (trans.), *Margins of Philosophy*. (Chicago: University of Chicago Press, 1982). p. 7.
10 J. Derrida, *Of Grammatology*. pp. 66-67.
11 J. Derrida, *Of Grammatology*. p. 5.
12 J. Derrida, *Of Grammatology*. p. 68.
13 J. Derrida, *Of Grammatology*. p. 69.
14 J. Derrida, *Of Grammatology*. p. 69.

Chapter 5: Spectral Matters

1   J. Derrida, T. Dutoit (trans.), *Aporias: Dying – awaiting (one another at) the "limits of truth"*. (Stanford: Stanford University Press, 1993). p. 12.

2   J. Derrida, *Aporias*. p. 20.

3   J. Derrida, *Aporias*. p. 15.

4   J. Derrida, *Aporias*. p. ix.

5   J. Derrida, *Aporias*. pp. 61-62.

6   J. Derrida, *Specters of Marx*. p. xviii.

7   J. Derrida, *Specters of Marx*. p. xix.

8   J. Derrida, *Specters of Marx*. p. xix.

9   J. Derrida, *Aporias*. p 21.

10   J. Derrida, *Specters of Marx*. p. xvi.

11   M. Heidegger, J. Macquarie & E. Robinson (trans.), *Being and Time*. (Oxford: Basil Blackwell, 1978). p. 284 (p. 240 in original German pagination)

12   J. Derrida, *Aporias*. p. 27.

13   J. Derrida, *Aporias*. p. 30.

14   J. Derrida, *Aporias*. pp. 57-60

15   This connection between death and memorialization also points to the important place of death with regards language in Heidegger and writing specifically in Derrida. In *Of Grammatology* Derrida specifically states that "all graphemes are of a testamentary essence" (p. 69) and with a reference to the Egyptian god Thoth, the god of both writing and death, he ties together graphic writing, the memorial of the pyramid and death. A triad that is repeated again in 'The Pit and the Pyramid: Introduction to Hegel's semiology' in *Margins of Philosophy*. And again in 'Plato's Pharmacy' in *Dissemination*. All this points further to the conjunction of writing as poison and *techne* as the death machine of experimental literature.

16   M. Heidegger, *Being and Time*. p. 294 (p. 250). Also quoted in J. Derrida, *Aporias*. p. 69.

17 M. Heidegger, *Being and Time*. p. 294 (p. 250).

18 J. Derrida, *Aporias*. p. 66.

19 The emphasis in this reading of death as the possibility of the absolute impossibility for *Dasein* highlights how authenticity and inauthenticity are inextricably bound together with regard to death and thus the rest of existence. Hence, it is only through an aporetic logic that the domain and limits of death can be mapped, such a logic is hauntology.

20 J. Derrida, *Aporias*. p. 35.

21 J. Derrida, *Aporias*. p. 61.

22 J. Derrida, *Specters of Marx*. p. 82.

23 J. Derrida, *Specters of Marx*. p. 82.

24 J. Derrida, *Specters of Marx*. p. 10.

25 J. Derrida, *Specters of Marx*. p. 86.

26 J. Derrida, *Specters of Marx*. p. 16.

27 See chapter 3 of *Specters of Marx* 'Wears and Tears (tableau of and ageless world)' for Derrida's breakdown and analysis just how out of joint the present world is; an analysis that has only become more evident in the intervening years since publication.

28 J. Derrida, *Specters of Marx*. p. 29.

29 J. Derrida, *Specters of Marx*. p. 5.

30 J. Derrida, *Specters of Marx*. pp. 157-158.

31 E. Laulau, 'The Time is Out of Joint' in *Emancipation(s)*. (London: Verso, 2007). p. 69.

32 J. Derrida, *Specters of Marx*. See all of chapter 5 'Apparition of the Inapparent: The phenomenological "conjuring trick."'

33 The schema set out here for delineating the domains of metaphysics draws upon that of Ray Brassier and the associated critique of conceptual idealism in his 'Concepts and Objects', in L. Bryant, N. Srnicek & G. Harman (eds.), *The Speculative Turn: Continential Materialism and Realism*. (Melbourne: re.press, 2011). The thinking of the so-called speculative realists has in many ways motivated this reading

of Derrida in terms of a spectral materialism, but it remains here only sketched out, incomplete and appropriately elliptical.

34   J. Derrida, *Specters of Marx*. p. 186.

35   J. Derrida, *Specters of Marx*. p. 189.

36   J. Derrida, *Specters of Marx*. p. 189.

37   M. Blanchot, 'Literature and the Right to Death', in M. Blanchot, G. Quasha (ed.), *The Station Hill Blanchot Reader*. (Barrytown: Station Hill Press, 1999). p. 386.

38   M. Blanchot, 'Literature and the Right to Death'. p. 386.

39   M. Blanchot, 'Literature and the Right to Death'. p. 378. The strong identification of Sade with this first slope of literature also accounts for the peculiarity of his will, as discussed in footnote 17 of *Aporias* pp. 86-87. Sade requests that when he dies he is buried in an unmarked grave scattered with acorns in an unknown forest, thus attempting remain only within the self-referntiality of writing and literature to escape the return to matter of second slope and maintain his commitment to absolute freedom.

40   M. Blanchot, 'Literature and the Right to Death'. p. 391. This is in fact a reiteration of a quote from Hegel, which appears several times throughout Blanchot's work. For a fuller account of the relation between Hegel, Blanchot and this particular quote, see: S. Critchley, *Very Little … Almost Nothing: Death, literature, philosophy*. (London: Routledge, 1997). p. 55.

41   S. Critchley, *Very Little … Almost Nothing*. p. 66.

42   S. Critchley, *Very Little … Almost Nothing*. p. 68.

43   M. Blanchot, 'The Instant of My Death.' p. 3.

44   M. Blanchot, 'The Instant of My Death.' p. 5.

45   M. Blanchot, 'The Instant of My Death.' p. 9.

46   M. Blanchot, 'The Instant of my Death.' p. 11.

47   T. McCarthy, *C*. (London: Jonathan Cape, 2010). pp. 187-190.

48   M. Blanchot, 'The Instant of my Death.' p. 7.

49 J. Derrida, 'Demure.' p. 112
50 J. Derrida, 'Demure.' p. 84.
51 For an example and summary of such a tendency see: A. Gallix (2011) *Hauntology: A not-so-new critical manifestation.* http://www.guardian.co.uk/books/booksblog/2011/jun/17/hauntology-critical?INTCMP=SRCH (last accessed 28/01/2012).

Chapter 6: Small Library Apocalypse
1 J. Derrida, 'Sendoffs', in, *Yale French Studies.* 77 Reading the archive: On texts and institutions, 1990.
2 J. Derrida, 'Sendoffs' pp. 15-16.
3 J. Derrida, 'Sendoffs.' p. 14.
4 J. Derrida, 'Sendoffs.' p. 33.
5 J. Derrida, A. Blass (trans.), *The Post Card: From Socrates to Freud and beyond.* (Chicago: University of Chicago Press, 1987). p. 11.
6 J. Derrida, *The Post Card.* p. 3.
7 J. Derrida, *The Post Card.* p. 6.
8 J. Derrida, *The Post Card.* p. 3.
9 J. Derrida, *The Post Card.* p. 62.
10 J. Derrida, *The Post Card.* p. 13.
11 F. Nietzsche, quoted in, J. Derrida, *Of Grammatology.* p. 6.
12 K. Siratori, *Blood Electric.* (www.creationbooks.com: Creation Books, 2002).
13 C. Tisdall & A. Bozzolla, *Futurism.* p. 89.
14 R. W. Flint (ed.), *Marinetti.* p. 41.
15 R. W. Flint (ed.), *Marinetti.* pp. 84-89.
16 J. Derrida, 'No Apocalypse, Not Now.' p. 30.

Chapter 7: The Work of Art and the Dangers of Technology
1 K. Ziarek, *The Historicity of Experience.* p. 44.
2 K. Ziarek, *The Historicity of Experience.* p. 44.
3 K. Ziarek, *The Historicity of Experience* .p. 45.
4 M. Heidegger, 'The Origin of the Work of Art', in, M.

Heidegger, D. F. Krell (ed.), *Basic Writings.* p. 210.

5   M. Heidegger, 'The Origin of the Work of Art.' p. 162.

6   M. Heidegger, 'The Origin of the Work of Art.' p. 161.

7   M. Heidegger, 'The Origin of the Work of Art.' p. 177.

8   M. Heidegger, 'The Origin of the Work of Art.' p. 179. Italics in original.

9   M. Heidegger, 'The Origin of the Work of Art.' p. 184.

10   M. Heidegger, 'The Origin of the Work of Art.' p. 191.

11   M. Heidegger, 'The Origin of the Work of Art.' p. 189.

12   M. Heidegger, 'The Question Concerning Technology', in, M. Heidegger, D. F. Krell (ed.), *Basic Writings*

13   M. Heidegger, 'The Question Concerning Technology' p. 324.

14   M. Heidegger, 'The Question Concerning Technology.' p. 325.

15   M. Heidegger, 'The Question Concerning Technology.' pp. 332-333.

16   M. Heidegger, 'The Question Concerning Technology.' p. 333.

17   M. Heidegger, 'The Question Concerning Technology.' p. 333.

18   M. Heidegger, 'The Question Concerning Technology.' p. 335.

19   M. Heidegger, 'The Question Concerning Technology.' p. 337.

20   M. Heidegger, 'The Question Concerning Technology.' p. 340.

Chapter 8: Only a Remembrance

1   M. Heidegger, 'The Origin of the Work of Art.' p. 166.

2   M. Heidegger, 'The Origin of the Work of Art.' p. 193.

3   D. Maleuvre, *Museum Memories: History, technology, art.* (Stanford: Stanford University Press, 1999). p. 2. See also T. W. Adorno, 'Velery Proust Museum', in, T. W. Adorno,

Prisms. pp. 175-185.
4   D. Maleuvre, *Museum Memories.* p. 23.
5   D. Maleuvre, *Museum Memories.* p. 50.
6   R. W. Flint (ed.), *Marinetti.* p. 42
7   R. W. Flint (ed.), *Marinetti.* p. 43
8   R. W. Flint (ed.), *Marinetti.* p. 43.
9   D. Maleuvre, *Museum Memories.* p. 51.
10 D. Maleuvre, *Museum Memories.* p. 10.

Chapter 9: Language, Literature and the Death Machine
1   M. Heidegger, 'The Way to Language', in, M. Heidegger, D. F. Krell (ed.), *Basic Writings.* p. 400.
2   M. Heidegger, 'The Way to Language.' pp. 408-409.
3   M. Heidegger, 'The Way to Language.' p. 414.
4   M. Heidegger, 'The Way to Language.' p. 420.
5   M. Heidegger, 'The Way to Language.' pp. 424-425.

Chapter 10: Death on a Pale Horse
1   J. Chapman, *Meatphysics.* (www.creationbooks.com: Creation Books, 2003).
2   J. Chapman, *Meatphysics.* p. ? (the last one).
3   J. Chapman, *Meatphysics.* Back cover.
4   M. Collings, *This Is Modern Art.* (London: Weidenfeld & Nicholson, 1999). p. 73.
5   M. Collings, *This Is Modern Art.* p. 73.
6   R. Hughes, *The Shock Of The New.* p. 20.
7   N. Rosenthal et al, *Apocalypse: Beauty and horror in contemporary art.* (London: Royal Academy of Art, 2000). p. 215.
8   N. Rosenthal et al, *Apocalypse.*
9   *Revelation.* (Melbourne: Text Publishing, 1998). p. 13.
10 M. D. Paley, *The Apocalyptic Sublime.* (New Haven: Yale University Press, 1986). p. 1.
11 E. Burke, quoted in M. D. Paley, *The Apocalyptic Sublime.*
12 I. Kant, W.S. Pluhar (trans.), *Critique of Judgement.*

(Indianapolis: Hackett Publishing Company, 1987).

13 J.-F. Lyotard, G. Bennington & R. Bowlby (trans.), *The Inhuman: Reflections on time*. (Cambridge: Polity Press, 1991). p. 90.

14 M. Heidegger, 'The Origin of the Work of Art.' p. 182.

15 J.-F. Lyotard, *The Inhuman*. p. 92.

16 There is an argument to be made here that the (mis)reading of Kant through Rimbaud's 'disorder of the senses' is symptomatic of what speculative realism calls correlationism. Such an argument could have serious implications for art as it resists the emphasis upon aesthetics, or sensibility at the expense of the object and the associated idealism that would reduce art to a mere image subject to the forces and discourses of the market or critical theory. The return to the spectral materialism developed in Chapter 5 and the associated critique of the commodity perhaps also suggests an interesting line for this argument to follow with regards to art.

17 J.-F. Lyotard, *The Inhuman*. p. 98.

18 J.-F. Lyotard, *The Inhuman*. p. 99.

19 J.-F. Lyotard, *The Inhuman*. p. 100.

20 M. Heidegger, 'The Origin of the Work of Art.' p. 201.

21 D. Maleuvre, *Museum Memories*. p. 65.

22 M. Heidegger, 'The Origin of the Work of Art.' p. 187.

23 J.-F. Lyotard, *The Inhuman*. p. 94.

24 M. Heidegger, 'The Way to Language.' p. 400.

25 M. Heidegger, 'The Way to Language.' p. 420.

26 J.-F. Lyotard, *The Inhuman*. p. 95.

Chapter 11: For the First Time and the Last Time

1 G.W.F. Hegel, quoted in, F. Jameson, *The Cultural Turn: Selected writings on the postmodern 1983-1998*. (London: Verso, 1999). p. 82.

2 F. Jameson, *The Cultural Turn*. p. 84.

3   J. D. Caputo (ed.), *Deconstruction in a Nutshell: A conversation with Jacques Derrida.* (New York: Fordham University Press, 1997). pp. 162-163.

4   J. P. Leavey Jr., 'Destinerrance: The apotropocalyptics of translation', in, J. Sallis (ed.), *Deconstruction and Philosophy: The texts of Jacques Derrida.* (Chicago: University of Chicago Press, 1987). p. 39.

5   J. P. Leavey Jr., 'Destinerrance.' p. 37.

Bibliography

Adorno, T. W., Weber, S. & Weber, S. (trans.), *Prisms*. (London: Neville Spearman, 1967).

Agamben, G., Binetti, V. & Casarino, C. (trans.), *Means Without End: Notes on politics*. (Mineapolis: University of Minesota Press, 2000).

Ballard, J.G., *The Complete Short Stories*. (London: Flamingo, 2002).

Blanchot, M., & Quasha, G. (ed.), *The Station Hill Blanchot Reader*. (Barrytown: Station Hill Press, 1999).

Bryant, L., Srnicek, N. & Harman, G. (eds.), *The Speculative Turn: Continential Materialism and Realism*. (Melbourne: re.press, 2011).

Caputo, J.D. (ed.), *Deconstruction in a Nutshell: A conversation with Jacques Derrida*. (New York: Fordham University Press, 1997).

Chapman, J., *Meatphysics*. (www.creationbooks.com: Creation Books, 2003).

Collings, M., *This Is Modern Art*. (London: Weidenfeld & Nicholson, 1999).

Critchley, S., *Very Little ... Almost Nothing: Death, literature, philosophy*. (London: Routledge, 1997).

Danto, A. C., *After The End Of Art: Contemporary art and the pale of history*. (Princeton: Princeton University Press, 1997).

Debord, G., Imrie, M. (trans.), *Comments on the Society of the Spectacle*. (London: Verso, 1990).

Derrida, J. & Dutoit, T. (trans.), *Aporias: Dying – awaiting (one another at) the "limits of truth"*. (Stanford: Stanford University Press, 1993).

Derrida, J., Blanchot, M. & Rottenberg, E. (trans.), *The Instant of my Death & Demeure*. (Stanford: Stanford University Press, 2000).

Derrida, J. & Blass, A. (trans.), *Margins of Philosophy*. (Chicago:

University of Chicago Press, 1982).

Derrida, J., Porter, C. & Lewis, P. (trans.) 'No Apocalypse, Not Now (Full Speed Ahead, Seven Missiles, Seven Missives), in, *Diacritics*. 14(2) Nuclear Criticism, Summer 1984.

Derrida, J. & Spivak C.G. (trans.), *Of Grammatology: Corrected edition*. (John Hopkins University Press: Baltimore, 1997).

Derrida, J. & Blass, A. (trans.), *The Post Card: From Socrates to Freud and beyond*. (Chicago: University of Chicago Press, 1987).

Derrida, J., 'Sendoffs', in, *Yale French Studies*. 77 Reading the archive: On texts and institutions, 1990.

Derrida, J. & Kamuf, P. (trans.), *Specters of Marx: The state of debt, the work of mourning and the new international*. (New York: Routledge Classics, 2006).

Derrida, J. & Blass, A. (trans.), *Writing and Difference*. (London: Routledge, 1978).

Docherty, T. (ed.), *Postmodernism: A reader*. (New York: Harvester Wheatsheaf, 1993).

Flint, R.W. (ed.), *Marinetti: Selected Writings*. (New York: Farrar, Straus and Giroux, 1972).

Fukuyama, F., 'The End Of History', in, *The National Interest*. Summer 1989.

Gallix, A. (2011) *Hauntology: A not-so-new critical manifestation*. http://www.guardian.co.uk/books/booksblog/2011/jun/17/hauntology-critical?INTCMP=SRCH (last accessed 28/01/2012).

Heidegger, M. & Krell, D.F. (ed.), *Basic Writings Revised and expanded edition*. (San Francisco: Harper Collins Publishers, 1993).

Heidegger, M., Macquarie, J. & Robinson, E. (trans.), *Being and Time*. (Oxford: Basil Blackwell, 1978).

Hughes, R., *The Shock Of The New: Art and the century of change, Updated and enlarged edition*. (London: Thames & Hudson, 1991).

Jameson, F., *The Cultural Turn: Selected writings on the postmodern 1983-1998*. (London: Verso, 1999).

Jameson, F., 'Future City', in, *New Left Review*. 21, May June 2003.

Kant, I & Fenves, P. (ed.), *Raising the Tone of Philosophy: Late essays by Immanuel Kant, transformative critique by Jacques Derrida*. (John Hopkins University Press: Baltimore, 1998).

Kant, I. & Pluhar, W.S. (trans.), *Critique of Judgement*. (Indianapolis: Hackett Publishing Company, 1987).

Klein, R., 'The Future of Nuclear Criticism', in, *Yale French Studies*. 97, 2000.

Laulau, E., *Emancipation(s)*. (London: Verso, 2007).

Light, M., *100 Suns*: 1945-1962. (London: Jonathan Cape, 2003).

Lyotard, J.-F., Bennington, G. & Bowlby, R. (trans.), *The Inhuman: Reflections on time*. (Cambridge: Polity Press, 1991).

Maleuvre, D., *Museum Memories: History, technology, art*. (Stanford: Stanford University Press, 1999).

McCarthy, T., C. (London: Jonathan Cape, 2010).

McNeill, W. & Feldman, K. S. (eds.), *Continental Philosophy: An anthology*. (Oxford: Blackwell, 1998).

Paley, M. D., *The Apocalyptic Sublime*. (New Haven: Yale University Press, 1986).

Revelation. (Melbourne: Text Publishing, 1998).

Rosenthal, N. et al, *Apocalypse: Beauty and horror in contemporary art*. (London: Royal Academy of Art, 2000).

Ruthven, K., *Nuclear Criticism*. (Carlton: Melbourne University Press, 1993).

Sallis, J. (ed.), *Deconstruction and Philosophy: The texts of Jacques Derrida*. (Chicago: University of Chicago Press, 1987).

Siratori, K., *Blood Electric*. (www.creationbooks.com: Creation Books, 2002).

Tisdall, C. & Bozzolla, A., *Futurism*. (London: Thames and Hudson, 1977).

Ziarek, K., *The Historicity of Experience: Modernity, the avant-garde and the event*. (Evanston: Northwestern University Press, 2001).

zero
books

Contemporary culture has eliminated both the concept of the public and the figure of the intellectual. Former public spaces – both physical and cultural – are now either derelict or colonized by advertising. A cretinous anti-intellectualism presides, cheerled by expensively educated hacks in the pay of multinational corporations who reassure their bored readers that there is no need to rouse themselves from their interpassive stupor. The informal censorship internalized and propagated by the cultural workers of late capitalism generates a banal conformity that the propaganda chiefs of Stalinism could only ever have dreamt of imposing. Zer0 Books knows that another kind of discourse – intellectual without being academic, popular without being populist – is not only possible: it is already flourishing, in the regions beyond the striplit malls of so-called mass media and the neurotically bureaucratic halls of the academy. Zer0 is committed to the idea of publishing as a making public of the intellectual. It is convinced that in the unthinking, blandly consensual culture in which we live, critical and engaged theoretical reflection is more important than ever before.